MW01103576

Melancholy, Mania and Miracles

Rachelle,
May God guide
your journey.
♡ Shelley

Melancholy, Mania and Miracles

My Journey with Bipolar Disorder

SHELLEY THODY

WESTBOW
PRESS
A DIVISION OF THOMAS NELSON

ISBN: 978-1-4497-7275-8 (e)
ISBN: 978-1-4497-7273-4 (sc)
ISBN: 978-1-4497-7274-1 (hc)

Library of Congress Control Number: 2012921301

WestBow Press books may be ordered through booksellers or by contacting:

WestBow Press
A Division of Thomas Nelson
1663 Liberty Drive
Bloomington, IN 47403
www.westbowpress.com
1-(866) 928-1240

Printed in the United States of America

WestBow Press rev. date: 12/6/2012

I dedicate this work to any of God's children who may feel lost, confused, terrified, and alone in their mental illness. *You* are not alone! I pray that through this book, with the help of loved ones around you and your own inner strength, you will be able to overcome your mental illness and live with light and love.

Contents

Foreword

My life became a little bit brighter on April 14, 1966, the day my little sister Shelley entered the world. She was a quite a bit different than me, all tiny and delicate, and I knew I would always need to protect her.

Growing up, she was driven in everything she did: exceptional grades in school, many different sports, and chores, just to name a few. "Perfection" was definitely in her vocabulary. She was also a very emotional child; I remember my dad could make her cry with just a look, so discipline was pretty easy. "Imperfections" in her looks were a big challenge for her; weight became an obsession at one point, her acne a never-ending struggle. These may sound like pretty normal behaviors for a young person, but the difference was that for her, everything was extreme. At this point, we as a family didn't recognize the signs, but looking back, they were definitely there, if ever so subtle.

Because of our age difference of three and a half years, she and I didn't hang out together much during our adolescence, so I don't recall too many examples of over-the-top behavior or depressions until she was in her late teens. For example, she talked about bizarre things or happenings; she talked so fast she would miss words and not make sense to anyone else; she was annoying to be around at times; and she thought God was talking to her through songs. This was our first glimpse into the manic side of bipolar disorder. Then, in natural succession, with bipolar disorder, after every high there is a low: depression! This is hard for someone on the outside to understand. I remember feeling like I wanted to shake her and tell her to smarten up, that things could not be that bad! I could not in my wildest dreams understand why she could not control the depression. This would be the start of our family being introduced to bipolar disorder, and the learning began.

Though her life was a series of ups and downs, she always had her family by her side. I believe having a close-knit family is one of the keys to successfully living with bipolar.

Shelley has become one of the most caring individuals I have ever had the pleasure to know. She is a loving wife, fabulous mother of three, and a veteran teacher. Her accomplishments are enormous—not to mention the phenomenal strength and courage she has facing this struggle everyday.

I wish you many, many more great accomplishments in your lifetime, little sister, and I know sharing this story is one of them.

Love, Roni

Preface

As I was flying alone to visit my parents in Arizona this past April, a voice said to me, "Make an outline!" I was just taking off from the Edmonton International Airport, and I thought, *What? Why? An outline ... for what?* But deep down inside, I knew exactly what God was asking of me. And unlike other times in my life, I decided to listen to his voice. Out came a pen and the back side of my previous night's hotel receipt, and I began outlining my life. I wasn't sure when I would find the time to write this book, but I knew God would find a way for me.

My name is Shelley Marie Thody, née Shelley Marie Ward. I am currently forty-three years old. I am married to a wonderful man named Dale, and I have three amazing children. Jamilyn is eleven; Kristy is eight; and Jesse is six. They are pure gifts from God and they continue to give and fill me up daily. My children fill me with love, purpose, humor, joy, and understanding. We can grow and learn so much from our children! I have a stepdaughter, Cindy, who is now twenty-two and lives in Texas. She has a little boy named Ryan, who is twenty months old. I guess, technically, I am a step-grandma! My husband, Dale, has met Ryan, but I haven't yet, although I really look forward to this. Many other people currently in my life will come up in the pages of this book as I write on, but this is my immediate family.

I am a teacher at a fairly large elementary school in northern Alberta. I currently teach grade one but have taught a variety of grades over the past fourteen years. I love teaching children. I enjoy the positive feeling of seeing children engaged, learning, and growing. I never thought I'd ever become a teacher. When I was a young child, I played "school" all the time and loved to pretend I was a teacher. However, in my adolescence, if anyone ever asked me, "What do you want to do when you get out of school?" I would merely respond, "Anything but be a teacher!" Why the dramatic shift? I didn't believe I could cope with four more years of schooling once I had completed high school. I have learned many things in my life, but first and foremost is that we should never limit our choices and always try to be open-minded. God often has a map for us that may not look anything like the one we have drawn for ourselves. It is when we decide not to listen to his direction that we find ourselves in the greatest trouble.

Because God led me to write this book, I believe his purpose is in providing light. Hopefully, by sharing my story, I may somehow help others gain hope and learn to survive in our chaotic, crazy world. I have bipolar disorder. I was diagnosed with this disorder back in 1986 and have been living with it for twenty-six years. It hasn't always been an easy road, but through God's guidance and grace, he has allowed me to live a fairly normal, healthy life. It is simply amazing to me when I look back on my life.

Chapter 1
My Normal Childhood?

You are my rock and my fortress. For the honor of your name,
lead me out of this danger.—Psalm 31:3 (The Living Bible)

When I consider my childhood, I realize now that although God is always with us, we often don't let him lead us …

I was born in Edmonton, Alberta, on April 14, 1966, at the Royal Alexandria Hospital. I had lots of dark hair and a scrunched-up face and was pretty funny-looking. I guess my mom and dad thought I was cute. When I was born, my sister, Roni, was three-and-a-half years old. We lived in St. Albert, just outside Edmonton. It was a nice neighborhood and a wonderful town to grow up in. We had many great, caring neighbors. There were so many friends close by for us children to play with. My younger sister, Tracey, came along a couple of years later, on June 6, 1968. We were three little girls growing up in a nice community with awesome parents who loved us very much. We were truly blessed. Mom took us to church on Sundays. When we were younger, we went to Sunday school, and once we were a bit older, we attended the church services at the St. Albert United Church. My dad didn't go to church except on special days like Easter or Christmas. I remember wishing he would come with us but not really knowing any different. It was a lot of work for my mom to get us up and to church on time. I am so glad she did! This was my foundation in Christ. This is where seeds were planted—a foundation that has had many layers, scuffs, scratches, and dents put into it over the years, but a foundation that has held me together in my toughest times.

My first obvious sign that God was watching me and wanted me to belong to this world a little longer was when I was thirteen months. My mom was busy when I went crawling into my room and somehow managed to pull the sliding crib rungs down onto my neck—back in 1966, safety standards weren't what they are today. My older sister, Roni, came into the house at that time and my mom asked her to check on me. She came back to my mom and said, "Shelley's asleep." My mom panicked as she knew I couldn't be sleeping so quickly. She frantically ran to me. I was blue in the face. She breathed into my mouth and ran with me to a neighbor, who was a doctor, and was home for lunch. They got me breathing, but the doctor asked my mom to take me into the general hospital in Edmonton. As if the trauma wasn't enough, my mom was questioned quite thoroughly about the incident in case she'd had any involvement. As a teacher and adult who has witnessed many awful, abusive homes, I can understand why they did this, and I am grateful. At the time, however, it must have been hard on my mom. They also checked my vitals, and I was soon released from the hospital. Thankfully, I was okay.

That was the *first* time Roni helped save my life.

At age five my life was again threatened. My mom and dad had taken us to Bawlf for the weekend to stay with Grandma and Grandpa Rhyason. My parents went to a convention in Medicine Hat. On Saturday, my sisters and I were in my grandpa's truck at the farm when we heard extreme weather warnings. Grandpa drove straight back to Bawlf and was met by my frantic grandma. Grandma had us all go sit in the hallway of their beautiful home. I knew something was wrong. I was scared and so were my sisters, but nobody really talked much. Soon, a horrible tornado hit Bawlf and the surrounding area. The winds were incredible and the sound daunting. Strange noises filled the air. Debris was flying everywhere. The sound of windows being smashed by golf-ball-sized hail was terrifying. We all sat huddled in the hallway, safe from any flying debris while my grandma and grandpa prayed in silence.

Finally, everything grew quiet and we stayed put while my grandparents went to assess the damages from this ravaging storm. A few minutes later, we were allowed to get up and look around. At that point in my life, I had no idea how violent and damaging Mother Nature could be. I really couldn't believe my eyes. My grandparents' yard was a disaster! Shingles, glass, and tree branches covered much of the yard. Luckily, the only damage to their house was to the windows and shingles. They were very thankful.

As we walked through this very small town, we saw that many people had not been as lucky. There was a great deal of damage. One huge tree across from my grandparents' house had to have been three feet in diameter, and it was snapped in two like a twig. A very unfortunate family who had lived close by on a farm was killed when this devastating storm picked up their house and tossed its precious belongings all over the place. It really was a horrific experience, one my family and I were lucky to have survived.

Was being in a tornado at such a young age a foreshadowing of my emotional future? A future of tumultuous feelings that may have been predicted by this crazy storm? Another thought I had was that this disturbance, once survived, again was a reinforcing factor that God would be watching over me through the storms in my life.

Life went on in St. Albert. I had many neighborhood and school friends. They often changed, but I always had someone. My sisters were friends too, and we enjoyed one another's company, most often when we weren't fighting. We are all so different yet so much the same. Aren't we all? We grew up skipping and playing hide-and-seek, red rover, and tag. In the winter, we built snow forts and went sliding and skating. We lived for outside adventures. My family often went camping in the summer. It was so much fun! I loved to play sports. When I was very young, my sisters and I started playing softball, though it wasn't the only sport I enjoyed; I had a true love for basketball. There is an ongoing joke in our house about this because I stand five feet zero inches when I stretch very tall. My husband still cannot believe I could have ever even made a basket, let alone played well at it! God gave me the ability to be fairly coordinated, fast, and very strong. I was blessed with encouragement from many people and involvement with basketball and softball from an early age. It was a true getaway and an oasis for me. I played basketball for six years and softball for about thirteen years.

Another wonderful retreat was playing the piano. I started about age seven and took lessons until sixteen. I still love to play. Piano is a nice getaway for me. Between sports, piano, church, and playing with my sisters and neighbors, school was a huge focus in my life. I loved to learn, be challenged, and always try my best. I loved the people in my life I met through school. Thanks to a combination of a supportive home, good teachers, and my dedication to hard work, I did really well in school.

It was important to me to do my very best in everything I did; sports was no exception, and basketball became a big part of my life during junior high school. I had many seven-in-the-morning basketball practices when my dad dropped my friend Molly and me off at our school. We would run stairs, up and down two flights, for fifteen minutes to start with and then continue with many other drills and exercises. It was all hard work, but to me it was worthwhile. Learning discipline in a different way helped me become stronger in many areas of life.

During my teen years, despite the positive influences of church, sports, family, friends, and school, I began to become unhappy with my weight. I was never a very big girl. In grade seven or eight, the most I weighed was about a hundred pounds. I was very short, so this was about average. I loved sports and was in fairly good shape. This particular age for girls is horrendous for many reasons. I liked my life; I loved my family; I loved my friends; I loved sports; I did very well in school, but I decided (or did the Devil in me decide?) that I didn't like my body. I was getting too fat for my liking. It was something to do with that magic one hundred number. Three digits! That *had* to be *big*! On top on all this, I have a mom who has always obsessed about her weight. Moms out there … all I can say is, if you don't like your own weight, try your hardest to do something positive about it and keep it to yourself! All my sisters and I heard all our lives was, "I'm so fat!" or "Look at me!" I would always reply, "Mom, you look great. I don't think you look big." But it was to no avail. Mom was always complaining and always dieting. She still is! *Be aware that our self-image is easily transferred to our children, even if it is not intended.* Often, I would go to the fridge to get a piece of fruit or something and I would hear, "Don't eat that. That is for our diet!" "Our" meaning my mom's and Roni's most often, unless Dad was "lucky" enough to be in on the latest diet craze . Roni had put on a bit of weight and wasn't completely happy with her appearance. However, having lived through this crazy food/diet-obsessed time in my family, I have come to realize and truly believe that *diets are insane*! Roni would merely sneak the things she was missing from her diet. I know this because I spent a lot of time with her in her room in those days. I was never surprised to see peanut butter sandwiches or chocolate bar wrappers. I wouldn't tell Mom. I mean, Roni was hungry! My mom wanted what was best for her and Roni, but it just wasn't working out.

What was God at this stage of their lives? I believed he was food. It was first and foremost in their minds and it took over. I know this feeling because around the same time, I started to think in a similar direction. I wanted to lose weight, exercise more, and be *thin*! Didn't every girl? Isn't thin still "in"? There are so many pressures for women to be "just so" in our culture. If only we can teach them to be just like God created them to be and not like some phony cover of a magazine!

But eating disorders go much deeper than the physical appearance so many strive for. For me it was mostly about control, I believe. I couldn't control my acne that I hated so much. I couldn't control my mom's negativity. I couldn't control my dad not being home much at night. I couldn't control my sister, Roni, and her habits. I *could* control my eating. Therefore, I did. I started to eat smaller portions. I started to skip meals. I exercised as much as possible. I would have something like a hardboiled egg for lunch. I would binge eat every once in a while and vomit. I hate to admit it, but I ended up bulimic for short period of time. I entered a new school, Paul Kane High School, for grade ten at a mere eighty-five pounds *thinking* I was fat. How does this happen? How does a well-adjusted girl get her mind so twisted into believing something that is not true? I believe the Devil takes over. I believe he has many times in my life, and probably yours too. I believe he constantly told me I was fat and needed to do something about it. I think he is my "negative self-talk." It is sad to think that all anorexic and bulimic people out there spend their entire day focusing on calories, food intake, and exercise. It is true. There is very little time to let anything else in. Food becomes your enemy and your God. What was created by God to allow us to live becomes what a person lives for. It was a sad and lonely existence. I didn't have any close friends at this time. I couldn't and wouldn't let anyone in. Was this truly the beginning of my struggle with mental health? I believe it was.

This downward cycle sometimes does not end. I was fortunate Roni noticed something was going on and how my weight continued to plummet. My mom probably thought it was all the sports and hadn't noticed much. Roni said something to my mom. My mom talked a bit to me about it, though I can't recall what was said. Not too long after, I began eating in a better fashion, though not completely cured of my problem. I had spent a great deal of junior high being the smallest and the tiniest. Somewhere inside I felt I had to keep this image up. For who? For what?

Was it helping me? Somehow, God's voice took over the Devil's inside me. Knowing how much my family cared for me gave me strength to get through this eating disorder. A few years later, this guiding voice inside me said, "Does your size really matter, Shelley? Doesn't God and your family accept and love you for who you are?" This was the beginning of the end of my obsession with weight and food. It was just not worth it! However, during this time of "weightlessness," something else happened in my life. I lost my periods. This was confusing and scary to me as I very badly wanted to have children sometime in my future,. Extreme weight loss will sometimes cause young girls to lose their periods.

By showing unconditional love and concern, this would have been the second time Roni helped save my life, as eating disorders can often lead to death, or at the very least take the life out of living. What an amazing sister! She's always loved me so much!

I would like to be finished with the "weight" topic, but there is more to say. We all know from Oprah and other sources that weight isn't about liking or disliking food. It goes so much deeper than that. I am not a psychologist, but I believe it was one of the early signs of my manic depression (as it was called many years ago). My mom and Roni had many conflicts and battles other than weight issues. They fought daily and fought a lot. Looking back, I believe Roni didn't like certain things about herself, and she took a lot of it out on my mom. I also believe my mom didn't like many things about her life at the time and took them out on Roni. Our house was living chaos some days. Many times I didn't even pay attention, as it had become quite common. I know now how much it really bothered me. I've always been a peaceful person who does not like conflict. I really try to love and not fight, trying my best to see the good in people. However, life isn't always like this, and I've come to know this firsthand now that my own daughter is approaching her teenage years. Many of her behaviors mirror that of my sister, Roni's. Many of my responses to my daughter, Jamilyn's, behaviors mirror that of my mom's. Life is scary sometimes! We cannot control most of life, yet we wish we could. Striving for that control on our own is fruitless. I had tried to find control through food. Reflecting now, I really wish I would have found it in God.

Controlling things was something I was still trying to do, however. As confusing as it sounds, I decided I would not behave like Roni. This decision may sound strange considering I idolized Roni, but I knew at this point in my life that I couldn't act like her. I decided to listen to my mom and to do as she asked. I would make my mom happy. It was a nice decision but possibly a bit self-destructive. A pleasing person often forgets what she wants or even likes in life. Was my weight loss in any way related to pleasing my mom? I'm really not sure, but it is quite possible. Such was my life at the time. My mom and I became close, and Roni and I became close too.

What about Tracey, my little sister? Well, Tracey did her own thing. I'm not saying these things did not affect her because I believe they must have. However, our cute little independent soul with a strong mind of her own had her own private way of dealing with things. When younger, Tracey and I shared a bedroom, played with Barbie dolls a lot, played house together, and we played with the neighborhood children and got along very well. Our only disagreement was who made the most mess in our bedroom and who should clean it up. She was very smart because once we decided to clean our separate halves, she merely pushed all of her stuff to my side of the room! Usually I just cleaned it up! Tracey approached the teen years with lots of friends and a private life that was separate from mine.

Again, reflecting on my teenage years, my weight had me obsessed, my family life was a bit chaotic, my older sister was beginning a life of partying, which worried me greatly, and I somehow had time for one more obsession—my acne! As I hit my grade six and seven years, I realized I could be quite anxious. I was jumpy at little noises and I had cold, sweaty palms most days. Whether it is this anxiety gene or another that causes acne, I'm not sure. I know that it runs deeply in my family, and I also know it is nasty. When I do meet with God in heaven one day, I have many questions for Him. There are many seemingly needless, hurtful things that many of us deal with on a daily basis. "Why does anyone have to suffer with acne? Why did head lice ever come to be? What good is psoriasis anyway?" But I also know that these questions could become much deeper and global such as questions regarding hunger, war, and suffering. My questions seem so minor compared to what many people deal with in life.

Whether I understand it or not, acne is something I've dealt with most of my life. I've had some form of pimples or acne for thirty-three years. To some of you reading this, you may be thinking, *So what? So you had a few pimples on your face? Get over it!* But the root of acne, for some, lies much deeper than the pores. I started with mere pimples on my face that I thought looked disgusting. As I matured, I ended up with cysts on my chin and ears and lots of acne on my chest and back. I felt like a freak! When many girls were excited to put on a new bikini and go to the beach, I wanted to hide under my clothes and cry. It certainly wasn't all about looks and vanity (although I have to admit that at that age, that was a factor). Instead, it was an obsession that began to take over a portion of my life, psychologically speaking. If worrying about your weight isn't enough, try adding in ugly pus-filled pimples over one third of your body! I spent *countless* hours in front of the mirror. I know. Now you are thinking, *Get over yourself!* No, it wasn't like that at all. My main purpose for the mirror was to wash, pick, squeeze, pick, wash, squeeze, scrub, cream, and cry. In the hours that sometimes passed, I now realize that I really was picking myself apart, literally. My hatred of my skin became a token of my self-acceptance. If I had pimples, I wasn't good. There was something very wrong. I remember crying often and saying things like, "I hate myself!"

Unfortunately, at that time in my life I was unable to accept myself the way God had made me. It makes me sad now. I know I'm not a beauty queen, but God made me with many admirable physical attributes like anyone else. When someone is inside herself with hatred, she really doesn't realize this at all. Many days I would become so upset that I would stand on my head for many minutes in a row. This actually helped me feel better. Maybe the blood supply going directly to the brain actually helped me cope a bit better. It also could have been my desire for mental balance by using my strong ability for physical balance.

For any of you who may suffer with eating disorders or acne, I pray for you. We don't know the reasons God gives us various things to deal with; we just must try to accept them and realize that lots of horrible things can help make you a better person. When I reflect about those times (as my skin is much better now), I deeply know that the experience I had as a teenager really helped me to empathize and deal fairly with others in this world. Have I ever called anyone fat? Have I ever mentioned that someone has a "pizza face" or laughed at somebody because of a scar or their height? No, I have never, and I stop anyone I see from doing it. I didn't need any bullies telling me about my face or back—I was the real bully. I bullied myself. That being said, if anyone did say something to ridicule me, I would bury myself deeper and deeper for a couple of weeks into my shell. I would scrub harder and try more creams and beat myself up a bit more for something I *truly* could not control.

With every little and big thing in life, God gives us hope, if we are willing to listen. My hope came from our little radio above our kitchen table one morning. I was listening to the news on our favorite radio station, when I couldn't believe my ears! Somebody had discovered a *cure* for acne! I jumped up, cheered, and screamed like I had just won an Olympic gold medal. Had I heard right? They said cure and not remedy? Believe me, at this point in my life (I was sixteen) I had tried *everything* for my acne—from antibiotics, creams, and cleansers to scrubs, masks, and sunlight. Many of these things helped a bit, but nothing actually took it away. Now my prayers were being answered. My mom and I were quick to act on this marvelous news. I went to my family doctor, who referred me to a dermatologist. The dermatologist warned me of the side-effects, sent me for blood work, and wrote me a prescription! Yes, finally the prescription to save my life! Not really, of course, but part of me was thinking just that at the time. The Accutane worked wonderfully. I did get a little dry in certain areas, but it really cleared up my chest, back, and most of my face. I was thrilled! I was seventeen years old at the time, and I was very happy!

God works in mysterious ways. Just as my skin was clearing up, another major thing was about to happen to my life. My dad came home from work one day, and we sat at the supper table to discuss an opportunity he had to transfer to Calgary, Alberta. Mom and Dad really wanted to know our (Tracey and me, as Roni had moved out on her own at the time) opinions. I remember thinking, *Cool! I've never lived anywhere else before. What an adventure! This will be so great!* I told dad that if it was better for him, I would be fine with moving to Calgary. Tracey felt a little sad and unsure. I had many great friends at the time, a serious boyfriend, and some wonderful neighbors. Still, it didn't seem to matter to me right then. I knew we had to go, but I was also very naïve.

Mom, Dad, and us girls helped pack everything up to go after having had a huge garage sale. Our special neighbors, the Moores, had a going-away party for us. Actually, they jokingly called it "The Neighborhood Improvement Party"! Mom and Dad left in the moving van first, and Tracey and I stayed at friends' houses, as summer had begun. Our plan was to meet in the middle the following weekend at our lake lot at Pigeon Lake. They would take Tracey and the car to Calgary, my boyfriend would pick me up, and I would head back to St. Albert to work at my part-time job for the summer at Dairy Queen. My close friend Molly and her family had offered to let me stay at their house for the summer while I worked and had my last fun times with my childhood friends. I was thankful to have my stay extended in St. Albert, to be with my friends a little longer.

The following weekend approached rapidly and I headed over to Tracey's best friend's house. Sandy and Tracey had been close friends and neighbors for many years. Once at Sandy's house, we shared an extremely tearful and emotional good-bye. We headed to Pigeon Lake and began a new chapter in our lives.

Chapter 2
Reality Sucks!

My enemies have chased and caught me. They have knocked me to the ground.—Psalm 143:3 (*The Living Bible*)

I'm sure Tracey and I cried halfway to Pigeon Lake, which is about one hour from St. Albert. Isn't this what we wanted? Isn't a change going to be good for us all? Why did our hearts ache so badly? Were we leaving our childhood behind? These questions buzzed around in our confused heads, and we were only two young teenagers with no answers. This *adventure* was going to be much harder than I had predicted! I guess I hadn't really considered the painful feelings in saying good-bye.

Once we arrived at our lake lot, we headed down to the beach to sit on the dock. It was a beautiful evening—calm, warm, and the sun was beginning to set over the water. It seemed to me as if the beautiful sphere was setting over my childhood as well. We continued to talk and cry. I do believe it was the beginning of a close friendship versus a sibling relationship between Tracey and me. The bond of conflicting emotions and uncertainty brought us together in a new way. We hurt so deeply, as if our hearts were being broken—not from a boy but by a place, a time, and relationships suddenly lost. The world as we had known it was gone.

My life changed on this very sad day in a significant way. Had I only reached out to God on that evening when I needed him so badly, I am sure that things might have turned out differently.

As we were brooding in our own little worlds, I noticed a group of older teenage boys close by, building a fire. Soon they asked, "Girls, do you want to come for a beer?" We just ignored them. Very soon after, we heard the same request but a bit more convincing. "Come on! Just come over and talk and have a beer!" It sounded very innocent, and Tracey, and I needed a little bit of cheering up. The temptation was there, and we were in great need of escape and comforting. Now, Tracey and I were not strangers to beer and alcohol in general. In fact, my family had been quite familiar with alcohol for many years—generations, in fact. My dad really liked to party but was always very friendly and never abusive, just very silly and then sometimes grumpy when he drank. My mom didn't drink very much when I was young as she had to take care of us kids.

My older sister, Roni, fell into the alcohol trap very tragically and easily. Roni began drinking at an early age and introduced me to the exciting effects of alcohol around twelve years of age. I was never a heavy drinker and didn't really like to get "drunk"; however, I was exposed to alcohol at a young age.

So, here we were, two despairing teenage girls whose lives felt like they are falling apart, and we heard some cute boys asking us over for a beer. Yes, we went over to talk and have a beer. At least that was our intention. As we got talking, we realized we had some personal connections. These guys were from St. Albert.

Keith was the cutest and he had this quiet, subtle, alluring way about him. He had long dark hair, beautiful, dark-brown eyes, and was in general very cute! Tracey's friend Sandy had been obsessed with his younger brother for many years. So we laughed and talked a bit about this. It so happened that Keith's older sister, Trina, had lived with Roni and a few guys a year before in a self-proclaimed "party house." Well, we had so much in common, and he was so sexy and I was so sad and ... yes, one beer led to another and another.

It seems fairly nice to leave our worries behind at times. Unfortunately, they always creep up tenfold the very next day. Tracey and I were having innocent fun, and yes, everyone was flirting somewhat too. As the fire grew hotter and the beer flowed easier, Keith leaned over and kissed me. It felt so right and so exciting! How could this older, gorgeous guy be liking me? I had an awesome boyfriend, Ben, at home. This wasn't like me at all! How could I do and feel such a thing for this guy? I felt so confused! Tracey was mad at me and giving me the "evil eye." I believe I had said something like this to her earlier: "Don't let me be stupid!" Unfortunately, a person has to control her own stupidity, and that night I was not really in control of anything other than wanting to feel good and taking the pain away.

The night wore on, and we were all getting pretty drunk. It started to get a bit cold, and the boys asked us to come back to their trailer. Innocently and with alcohol-induced stupidity, I said yes. Tracey came along too with one of the guys' arms around her. I really don't know what I expected at the trailer. Maybe a game of cards? Some hot chocolate possibly? *Come on, Shelley; deep down you knew what you were possibly getting yourself into, didn't you?* I really can't say, but I should have known better. Once we arrived at the tent trailer, Tracey and her beau went to one bed, and we started necking on the other. What a positive, older sister role model I was that night! Unfortunately, many times in my life I was far from being a good role model for my little sister. I am truly sorry, Tracey. One thing led to another on that trailer bed, and soon Keith's intentions became very clear!

I had gotten myself into a situation that was not easy to back out of.

A while later, Tracey and I sneaked back to our trailer and tried to fall asleep. Tracey knew what had happened and tried to talk to me. I just needed to weep. I didn't go to sleep, and the next day Mom and Dad would be there. How could I face my parents? Wouldn't they know right away? What could I say? Where could I hide? What if we saw those boys again today? I wanted to curl up into a ball and hide away. I was supposed to head back to St. Albert. How could I face Ben? I was heavily beating myself up. My mind-set was beginning to change about who I was and where I was going in life. My emotional state added with alcohol had turned out to be a poisonous mix.

Ben was coming to pick me up in a few hours.

Life goes on, however, even when sometimes we wish it wouldn't. Mom and Dad arrived, happily and busily trying to get a few things accomplished at the lake. I really don't think they noticed anything at all different or wrong with their little girl. I always wanted to be an actress! Ben had arrived punctually a little while later, and I performed again. Soon it was time for our tearful good-byes, and I headed off with Ben to St. Albert for the summer. I was feeling confused and guilty, but I wasn't about to share this information with Ben.

The summer was very busy. My friends and I cruised in Molly's little Datsun to the beat of "Africa" and "Walking on Sunshine." I worked, went to the beach, saw Ben quite a bit, hung out with my friends, and tried to forget what had happened at the lake. I began to distance myself from a relationship with God around this time.

Summer came and went quite quickly, and it was time for me to head to Calgary for good. When the day came to say good-bye to Ben, it was easier than I thought it would be. Don't get me wrong; he was a great guy! He was very cute—blond, blue-eyed, awesome, sporty figure, lots of fun, and very intelligent (he went on to become a lawyer); but something told me it wouldn't last. He felt the same. We were young and had many years ahead of us. I think we were just being mature and somehow understood that our futures were not meant to be together. We had a big hug, a few tears, and said "so long and good luck!" I think about Ben often and pray he is doing well in his life. He helped me grow and learn many things about myself. Saying good-bye to my friends was very similar. We wouldn't lose touch, and we would write many letters. Life would go on as normal ... only long distance.

Saying good-bye wasn't as hard as I thought it would be. Plans had been set that I would be back to celebrate Paul Kane's High School grad the following May. After all, I had been with these friends all my life and would want to celebrate this huge event with them. Now I was heading into a new, huge school, going into grade twelve, feeling all alone.

Was the schooling somehow something I had not considered? Was I so naive that I thought everyone would just open their arms welcoming Tracey and me into a new, gigantic, scary school? I guess sometimes ignorance is bliss. Henry Wisewood High School was anything but welcoming. It was plain scary! I thank God I had Tracey with me, and am sure she feels the same. This huge school of six hundred-and-some students had a "clique" for everything except us! There were the "jocks," the "heads (drug-users)," the "geeks," etc., and then there were two new scared girls. We both smoked at the time, so we would meet at the smoking area and try to find refuge in our cigarettes. It was quite ironic to hear someone calling my name one day. I looked to see Robyn running toward me from down the hallway. Robyn and I had been on the same drill/dance team, called the "Stars of St. Albert." We had performed cheerleading-type dance at various venues such as opening ceremonies and pre-game/halftime shows at Edmonton Eskimo games. So here I was amidst so many strangers and saw a familiar face calling my name. I was so excited. We hugged, talked, and made plans to meet. She soon introduced me to another girl also named Tracey and also from St. Albert. My sister Tracey and I finally had a group and felt like we belonged a bit more.

One nice thing about *not* knowing many people in your grade twelve year is that you can really concentrate on your studies. My marks were awesome! I still found time to have fun. Tracey and I hung out with Robyn and Tracey quite a bit and found a few good parties to go to on the weekends.

As an aside … and not meaning to pull you out of the past, but right now I am in the midst of a depression and am hurting. Sometimes the truth comes out much more easily if we are really feeling the pain. I have been in a depression for about three weeks. This is odd for me because I really am normally controlled with my current medication. I have experienced a couple to three "down" days from time to time, but this is more extreme for some reason. My school teaching year has started. I have had to move classrooms again (I had two moves this year, two moves last year), which is a major endeavor. Thankfully I had some help from my nephew Trevor this year and my dad and husband last year. Moving classrooms really involves a lot. A teacher has all her personal binders, folders, cabinets, desk items, bulletin board items, cleaning items, boxes of decorations, etc. It really is a big deal and a major amount of extra time. However, I persevered and was ready, with their help, for my class this year—physically ready with my class, but not as emotionally and lesson-ready as I would have liked after spending so much time on the move.

About one week into school, my family started getting sick. Along with rest, antibiotics, and nebulizers, they soon got better. I also began to get physically and mentally sick the first week in September. It is now September 29 and I have been holding it together on the outside. I still was able to teach, plan, make up my IPPs (individual program plans), make it to meetings, and call parents. However, at night, many, many tears have fallen. I am barely managing to cope. I have a light cluster headache in the base of my brain radiating out hopelessness, frustration, fear, and tears. I have increased my medicine a bit, which normally helps. However, because I am also physically sick, I find it extra difficult to cope. Life is about balance, and when you have two major things running against you, this balance is definitely broken. Sinus infections, throat infections, etc. are my common affliction. Yes, again, silent pain. It is interesting that my life carries so much silent pain. If you are reading this, I would imagine that yours does as well. Silent pain is interesting. It becomes apparent if you share it with someone but otherwise merely eats you up inside while you attempt to cope. With an infection, you can get an antibiotic, but with depression, things are always more complicated, especially with bipolar people.

One thing I really wanted to get across is my idea of "brain infection." I know it sounds ridiculous, but when I am physically sick in my head, I really feel at least a little depressed. Maybe all people do when they are sick. I have a very difficult time thinking clearly. This time, due to various chemical and/or situational things going on in my life, my depression is running deeper. I lose a lot of my coping skills, get easily frustrated, and sometimes yell at my children (which I absolutely hate and ask God for forgiveness and redemption every time). Okay, so now you have a person who is physically, mentally, and emotionally ill because she is upset about the way she is behaving. Is it ever going to end? *Yes!* I know it is because in the midst of my horrible day as I write, I know there will be some light and that some people really care about me, that I do make a difference somewhere, and that we all make mistakes. I have gotten through much worse than this and survived. There is always hope ... do not give up on your rough days! Instead, try harder to at least cope with the things you can. It often makes me slow down when I have an infection. There is more time to sit on the couch (something I don't do very often). Therefore, there is more time to snuggle with my children, talk to them, read them a story, or have them read to me—a perfect example of some light. If we are willing to see, God always will provide us with some light, even in our toughest battles.

That being said, an interesting thought came to me this morning. A lady in our school was approximately six months' pregnant. Over the weekend, her water broke and she was rushed to the Royal Alexandria Hospital in Edmonton. Thankfully, she and the baby are okay, but she is on bed rest until the baby is due. She will have to stay in Edmonton for a while and be monitored.

All our prayers are with her and her family, and we are all quite concerned.

Yesterday after school many teachers met to discuss how we can help Trina and her family. I didn't meet, though I plan to help and have already e-mailed her with my concern and prayers, despite feeling so rough by the end of yesterday. Instead, I came home to my family and flopped on the couch in tears of frustration. The interesting thing isn't that people are busy planning something to help a family in need. That is a very caring, Christian thing to do. What I was thinking about this morning was that I have been in pain for three weeks in that same school, and I know I wear my heart on my face. I am just that way. Only three people on our staff have even talked to me about it in any way. Most wouldn't know or care that I am in a depression right now. Really, what is so different? Isn't Trina going through a difficult emotional time right now? Well, Shelley is going through a difficult emotional time right now and has been for three weeks!

I know it may even sound selfish, but I really don't think it is. We need to be recognized for the pain and suffering that *we have no control over,* or we certainly wouldn't feel this way at all. Depression is a private and deep issue, but a person really needs a shoulder, an ear, or a kind word of encouragement every once in a while to help her through. Mental health needs better understanding in general. I guess too it has made me want to feel more aware of others' emotional hurts and to try my best to never dismiss them. There is certainly a social stigma around depression and mental illness in general. It seems easy to talk to someone if he or she has a bad cough, cold, or broken bone. However, if someone is clearly depressed or showing signs of mental illness, we tend to ignore it or at least avoid the person. I also believe the person dealing with the mental illness needs to begin to open up and be honest about the way he or she is feeling. Maybe the response to, "How are you today?" should honestly be, at times, "Not very well, actually. I feel depressed and overwhelmed today." Only through being truthful and receiving compassion from others can we start to break this chain of indifference.

I will continue to pray and help Trina and her family out financially too. She is a kind, sweet, giving person who deserves nothing but a healthy child to love. I will continue to pray for people caught in the grips of depression that they too will find that healthy child full of light inside themselves.

Early in my grade twelve year, I was invited to a party. Tracey and I decided it would be fun to do something different and to meet new people.

After being at the party for about an hour, I glanced over and saw a very cute boy across the room. He smiled seductively smile at me. He had green eyes, light–brown, wavy, long hair, and was very tall. Again the Devil had tempted me and I jumped at the bait. Soon, Mark Jones walked across the room and we were talking. I don't really think Mark was the Devil. Many of the things he was influenced by were extremely dark, though. All I saw that night was hope for a new boyfriend! I needed company, closeness, and love, and he was really gorgeous! Of course he was also very friendly that night. Mark asked me if I wanted to go on a date and I replied, "Sure!"

What was I getting myself into? It seemed exciting at the time. Our first date was meeting at the LRT station (Mark didn't drive) and going to South Centre for a pop and a visit. It went very well, and our relationship quickly progressed. We called one another often and saw each other at least twice weekly (me always driving). Our relationship was nice and very physical at first. Mark said he loved me and I think he did in his own way. I thought I loved him too. The excitement and fun of our new relationship was influenced greatly by his friends, drugs, and alcohol. I never did drugs or wanted anything to do with drugs and suddenly I found myself going out with a druggy! I didn't fully realize this at first. In fact, I remember the guy who had had the party, Alf, phoned me one day to warn me about Mark. He didn't think too highly of him, and I don't think Mark had even been invited to the party. Alf said Mark was always partying, was in trouble at school, and he didn't trust him. When I look back on that call, I have to appreciate the efforts made by Alf. However, as the Devil was in greater control of my life at this point, it really didn't matter what he told me. I was head over heels in trouble and lust. It soon became apparent what our relationship was going to look like. I would pay, drive, and be the responsible one. Mark would party, get drunk and stoned, take advantage of me in various ways, and control me when he could. How stupid was I anyway?

I soon had warnings from my sisters and friends. My dad even stayed up one night when I was out late. He got really mad at me and grounded me! That had never happened before! I was always the good girl. I do know my dad's discipline that night had some impact on my future decision about my relationship with Mark Jones. We definitely need loving boundaries as teens even though we try to fight them. God often works through the ones we love to help us see things clearly. Looking back I see this clearly, but in the midst of being a teen in an abusive, lusty, confusing relationship, I didn't seek God's help and didn't realize at the time that he truly was helping me and guiding me closer to him.

Mark had a history, as we all do. My heart went out to him greatly. When he was only thirteen years old, he found his mom dead on the couch. I can't even imagine! I never learned the details or circumstances leading to her death. At that time in my life all I could really think of was, *Poor Mark, I need to help him.* His brother was a bully who beat on Mark a couple of times while we were going out. His dad was an alcoholic and probably an abuser too. I know in my heart I really did want to help Mark. I just wasn't in any position to do that, so I tried by loving him. He needed help much greater than I was able to offer him.

With so many emotional, psychological, and drug-induced issues, Mark made many mistakes. He abused drugs and alcohol to try to conquer his pain. He skipped school often and stole things to help pay for his destructive habits. Many "dates" would consist of my sitting in a hazy basement with Mark and his three doper friends and watching them get high. What young love endures! Unfortunately, I was convinced to try a couple of different drugs from time to time. I tried acid, mushrooms, and marijuana. I never liked the feeling of being high for the most part. I only tried these drugs about a total of five times, and I wish I hadn't at all. Why do we try to alter our reality so much? Why did I risk hurting the body God gave me? I didn't think of these things at all when I was eighteen. I just wanted to fit in with my boyfriend's crowd. Looking back, I realize I could have easily become a real drug addict. God was again pulling me his way. He started to work on me through questioning my relationship with Mark.

I was accepted into the pharmacy technician program at Red Deer College and started to set some positive goals for myself. My auntie Doris and uncle Stan Thorn were so generous to allow me to stay at their house for the year. My relationship with Mark became long distance and probably was the onset of his extreme jealousy. I loved college and worked very hard. The course was compact, with lessons and labs all crammed into a short period of time. I came home by bus many weekends to spend time with my family and Mark. Mark came to Red Deer a couple of times too.

The Thorn family was amazing. At the time, my cousins Marvin and Greg were left home. My older cousins had already moved out. Everyone made me feel at home and special. I was given special privileges, like driving my auntie's car when Marvin (who is the same age as me) wasn't allowed to. I don't think he liked that too much! Marvin, Greg, and I got along great, and Marvin was going to the same college as me. I would walk to school, but on cold days, Greg would often pick me up to drop me off. I made some great friends, learned a lot, and really had a great experience going to college. Marvin and I went to a couple of parties together. It was all innocent fun. The year was so busy and really zoomed by. I graduated and was now ready to look for work. I said some tearful good-byes to my aunt, uncle, cousins, and friends and moved back to Calgary to my parents' place.

Once I came home, I soon realized that my relationship with Mark was much less fun and much more argumentative. He didn't want me to enjoy life. If we went to a bar, I would stay sober to drive while he would get smashed. I would ask him to dance and he wouldn't, and he refused to let me dance with anyone else. He was becoming more and more jealous and somewhat abusive too. One night, as we were leaving the backseat of my sister's car, he spit on my hair. This didn't register with me, but Roni was really angry at him. Roni and Ken had just moved to Calgary into an apartment. Roni and I talked lots that night, and I started to realize I didn't need him in my life. Deep down inside I was afraid to break up with him. Naively, I didn't fear what he might physically do to me but what might become of him.

From somewhere deep inside I found enough courage to go over to his house. I said something to the effect of, "Mark, I am so sorry, but this isn't working for us. I can't go on like this. I need to break up with you." Right away he started crying. I felt horrible and started to cry too. He said, "I'll change. I'll get a job and stop the drugs!" All I said was that I am sorry, and I hugged him and left. I cried all the way home. I had found the courage to let him go and knew I had made the right decision. God bless you, Mark Jones. I often say prayers for him.

Right around this time, I went to Arizona on a holiday with my mom, dad, Roni, brother-in-law, and nephew, Trevor. Trevor was just nine months old and so cute! I've always craved the sun, and whenever I've been able to combine sunshine and a holiday together, it would make me extremely blissful. We stayed in a motel and visited my grandparents at their trailer park. The sun, company, and relaxation were great and felt wonderful!

Whenever I started to feel elated, my speech would immensely change. Basically I could talk really fast! It all made sense to me, but not always to everyone else. On this holiday, I would wake up really early (which was common for me anyway) and take Trevor for walks. One time we were heading for Dunkin' Donuts, and a lady said to me, "What a cute baby you have!" I just smiled and said, "Thanks!," not admitting he wasn't really mine!

One evening my brother-in-law, Ken, and I were on a quest for Mexican food. There was a take-out place across the street. I love Mexican and couldn't wait! As we were crossing our parking lot to head to the restaurant, a young Mexican man was heading our way, a brown bag in his hands. We said hi and stopped to talk. Ken mentioned that we were headed to get some food. This guy said that the restaurant had just closed. I was really disappointed. Where were we going to find Mexican at this time of night now? I went on babbling to this young guy for quite a while about who knows what.

After a few minutes, he looked me right in the eyes and asked, "What was your name?"

I responded, "Shelley."

Then he quite forcefully replied, "Chelly, chut up!" I just laughed! But not as much as Ken did! I'm sure Ken wanted to tell me exactly the same thing more than once on this holiday!

Anyway, this man ended up giving us his Mexican food that he was taking back to his fiancée! He made a deal with us that he'd come over for a drink later. We were soon to be leaving and had a bunch of booze to drink before we left. It seemed like a good idea at the time. Mexican food and a party! Well, Roni couldn't believe our story when we got back to the room. Soon after eating, this guy showed up at our room. We all had a few drinks and realized there was more to the bargain than just Mexican food. He was after me too! We tried everything nice to get rid of him, but it just wasn't working. The guy had a fiancée a few doors down! Finally, after he'd had too many drinks, we convinced him the back door was the washroom, and we quickly locked the door behind him. It was a very interesting night!

As I recall this trip to Arizona, I realize now that the hyperactive talking, elated feeling, and very little sleep was probably my first experience of being in a mild manic high.

Once back from Arizona, I started searching for a job in the Calgary phone book and called many pharmacies. Nobody seemed interested in hiring a technician. Many didn't even know the job existed. However, through perseverance, on my third day of calling pharmacies, I encountered a kind lady by the name of Flo. She said she would like to meet me and maybe work something out. I was so excited! At least this was a start. The next day, I went to MacGlen Pharmacy to meet with Flo. She was kind and inquisitive. I think she knew my whole life in half an hour! She asked me what I was capable of doing. She said she was becoming very busy in the pharmacy and could use some help. She hired me that day, and I was so excited!

Everything in my life was coming together! I had come home to the family I loved so much. I had bravely broken up with a boy who was not good for me. I had graduated from college and now had an actual full-time job as a pharmacy technician! Wow! Life couldn't get better! Unfortunately, this small "high" didn't last too long, and my life began to take on drastic changes.

Chapter 3
The Color Blue

That is why I wait expectantly, trusting in God to help,
for he has promised.—Psalm 130 (*The Living Bible*)

My job was really okay. Flo was great to me. She treated me like the daughter she never had. She bought me lunch almost every day. She found me many menial tasks to do to keep busy. The pharmacy wasn't as busy as she had indicated. I was placing stock, shelving magazines, and dusting. But I wasn't filling prescriptions like I wanted to be doing. I didn't feel like I was using my training at all. On top of all of this, Mark found out where I was working and would periodically show up asking to have another chance. I was suddenly miserable in my work life, personal life, and now that I reflect, in my spiritual life too. Where was my purpose? Why was I feeling so blue? Why did I not want to get up in the mornings? These questions and others started to haunt me. I just wasn't a happy young girl of nineteen anymore.

My mom started to worry about me. She talked to a lady and made me an appointment with a doctor to discuss what was happening to me. When I went to the first appointment, the doctor merely dismissed my symptoms and said to my mom that often young adults go through a time of feeling blue when there is lots of change. My mom knew me well and understood that it was definitely not like my personality at all to be behaving and feeling this way. I found it hard to get out of bed in the mornings and to look myself in the mirror. I pushed myself anyway and always showed up for work, although I cried my way there many days. Here I was, an adult with a career and a loving family, but inside I felt very much like a little needy baby. Why? Why was I feeling so utterly blue and useless? I wasn't sure where to turn.

Thankfully, the love of God through many people in my life helped me cope with this low-scale depression, as I now see it. Flo was so good to me and very loving. She must have known something was wrong, but she didn't know me well enough to know much different. My mom, dad, and sisters were amazing as always and continued to encourage me. Dad and I hadn't had many heart-to-heart talks up until this point in my life.

I remember him coming into my room early one evening and sitting on my bed with me. He knew I was very sad and discouraged. He said, "What's wrong, Shelley?"

I responded something to the effect of, "I'm a loser and can't think properly. I feel stupid and don't like myself!" Then I started to bawl.

He hugged me and was very frustrated with me. He replied with his arm around me. "Don't be ridiculous! You're beautiful, smart, and wonderful. You've finished college, and you have a great job. You have so much going for you. I love you!"

I had longed for words like these to come from my dad for many years. He came from a wonderful, funny, friendly family. His family didn't share emotion very much though. It wasn't easy for my dad to let his heart out in the open. So here I was with my dad showing me great love and understanding, and I couldn't believe a word of it. I felt that bad about myself. Don't be fooled. Kind words go a long way and travel for many years. Maybe that day I couldn't believe what my dad was saying or even feel that I deserved them. Maybe, though, they resonated deep in my soul and began a slow healing process of this particular depression. Never be afraid to express love and compassion to one another. We all need it!

I went on feeling miserable for a few more weeks, but I started to feel a bit more hopeful. Then a phone call to my parents' home one evening sparked something in me that set my life in a new spin.

Chapter 4
Kite Flying

He lets me rest in the meadow grass and leads me beside the quiet streams. He restores my failing health.—Psalm 23:2–3 (*The Living Bible*)

Again, I must pause in my reflections on the past and flash forward to my life at the present. I feel it is only fair to share with you the constant reality of dealing with a mental illness. It is the beginning of February, and it is usually a tough time in my cycle (late January to mid February). Is it my location? I am quite far north and see little sunlight during the winter. Or is it just my system? I am not sure, but regularly at this time of year I find my moods very difficult. I am able to cope but it is more challenging. That being said, I have had a major change occur over the last two months. In late October, my pharmacist pulled me aside and asked me if I am still taking Duralith. I replied yes, and he proceeded to tell me that it is being discontinued. At first I couldn't believe my ears. Discontinued? How can they do this? It is a vital aid in many peoples' lives, including mine. It has helped me stay sane and functional for the last twenty-two years! What was he telling me? I felt a small sense of panic. I asked my pharmacist why.

He replied, "If it isn't making money, they just stop making it!"

It was disheartening to hear this. Some things in life shouldn't be about the almighty dollar. We all know differently, though. I also thought in the back of my mind that regular Lithium was still available. However, I have tried this type before, and it hadn't worked the same for me as the sustained-released (Duralith) Lithium. I knew that I would have some work ahead of me. Should I search the continent for remains of Duralith? What would be the point. I'd only be prolonging the inevitable.

Instead, I prayed to God to help me, and I began my search for alternatives. I went on the Internet and searched "bipolar + treatments." I came across a couple of things. One medication claimed to "cure" bipolar within two to three months! Please, please, please I prayed … but if you suffer with this disorder, *do not ever believe that*! I knew it was too good to be true.

In the meantime, I was talking to Tracey, and she mentioned that she worked with a girl who is taking "Power Plus minerals." I went onto the Internet and did some heavy research on this vitamin/mineral-based therapy. After much deliberation, reading testimonials, and praying, I decided that this product sounded well researched and would definitely be worth trying. I talked to people working in the company as they have a very good support group to help people with weaning off one or more drugs and introducing the product.

December 22 was the day I started taking Power Plus while still on some Lithium. I weaned off the Lithium over about three to four weeks until I was just on Power Plus. At first it seemed to be working okay. I didn't feel too much different. I was able to function well. I didn't feel any major blues or highs. However, as time went on, I started to feel quite different. I was getting severely anxious. I couldn't breathe properly. I had a big lump in my throat and chest. I had high blood pressure and could hear my blood pumping behind my ears. I was retaining a lot of water, which is always a sign for me of impending mental illness. After talking to a consulting nurse, I decided to add another pill as I wasn't at full capacity, according to their protocol.

However, I've never needed to take as much medication as most people to get full effects of any drug. This addition of an extra capsule only made things worse. What was I going to do?

My old form of lithium was gone. This *true hope* of mine was disintegrating before my eyes. Even though my psoriasis was finally healing, and I was thinking a bit more creatively and clearly, I was falling apart inside. What was my next step going to be?

After talking to my mom and dad and finally telling them what I was doing, I did some more soul searching. They were very scared. They know how well Lithium had been working for me through the years. I was also scared and unsure. I got even sicker and was unable to sleep for an entire night. This is a sure sign for me of triggering a manic high. I felt so uptight and cranky! I decided to see a doctor. Timing in life is everything. My husband, Dale, called my doctor at home as he had just begun a month of holidays. He directed Dale to make me go to the hospital that night to see someone. Last night, that is exactly what I did. In more than twenty-two years, I had never gone to the *hospital* for anything related to bipolar. It was very difficult. I live in a very small community. But it was necessary. I had too much at stake. My family was counting on me. My students and friends were counting on my recovery. God mostly was counting on me. It was soon apparent at the hospital that the doctor on call was someone who isn't always respected in our community. However, my path had led me to him.

In my desperation and faithfulness, I turned to my *real* true hope and said a prayer. "God please allow me to leave behind my past experiences and assumptions about this man. Please allow me to meet him with an open mind and heart and to speak about my situation honestly. Please soften his heart and allow him to help me with my mental disorder."

I saw this doctor in a different light. He was a real, caring, honest-to-goodness person. He really listened and tried his best to help me. He sent me home with the direction to go back on Lithium (regular) right now and to slowly increase the dosage. I was asked to see him again in a week, and he would promptly make an appointment with a psychiatrist. We may then discuss another route, or possibly find a Lithium regimen that will work for me. I stayed home from school to write this. It was a *true* mental health day. I was still not breathing properly. I have a lot of built-up anxiety. My hopes were smashed in something new, but I have not given up. I went for a serene, beautiful walk alone this afternoon through the forest. The sun came out for the first time in at least a week (a rare thing in Alberta to not have a lot of sun). I saw hope and knew the path God was leading me on has many bumps, turns, and snags. I must be strong and persevere on my hardest days. God is good!

Living with a condition such as bipolar in a small town hasn't been easy. It has constantly been a combination of trying to stay healthy while attempting to live in secrecy. There was a time I would drive to a small town nearby or go to Calgary to fill my prescriptions. This was quite stressful. There are so many people who do not understand this mental illness at all and who have a preconceived idea about what bipolar disorder is all about. I felt years ago that my career and credibility would have been threatened if the truth was told. Throughout the years, I have grown and trusted certain people in my community. I now get my prescriptions filled regularly by a variety of people without feeling anxious at all.

A month has passed, and I am taking Lithium regularly and have reached a positive, healthy dose. It appears that this will be my answer, again, after all. Even in the different delivery system, Lithium is working for me to keep me human, sane, functioning, loving, and thankful! I do have my psoriasis back again, but my sleep, sanity, and functionality is so very much more important right now. I thank God every day for helping me, again, through a very tough time. It is a terrifying thing for someone with a mental disorder to try a new medication. I felt I had no choice at the time as my medication was discontinued, but the justified fear is very hard to explain. The memories of my terrifying past came intensely back to me. Nobody wants to lose the control they've struggled so desperately for in the past. Some questions that enter my head now are, "Did God direct me to try Power Plus? Did he know it wouldn't work for me? Did he want to reinforce one last time how very important Lithium is for my condition of bipolar? Did he need me to pass on this important message to others?" Of course I don't know these answers for certain, but God directs us in many ways. He knows our strengths, weaknesses, and capabilities. He guides us if we are willing to be guided. We always get stronger and wiser through our suffering.

The phone call came from Harvey, a wonderful pharmacist/owner of Shoppers Drug Mart in St. Albert. I had done my retail pharmacy practicum in St. Albert during my pharmacy technician program. I had really enjoyed it at the Shopper's because it was busy and very much hands-on. I was actually a *technician* when working there, not a shelf organizer. Harvey called and said his store was becoming even busier, and he was considering hiring a technician to help out in the pharmacy. "Are you interested in the job, Shelley?"

We hashed out the details and the pay, and I responded in a very excited, "*Yes*, I will take the job!"

It was amazing! I would have a chance to work in a real, busy pharmacy and move back to St. Albert where I belonged! My life was taking a positive turn, and I felt so good inside.

I was so excited and ready to go back "home" to St. Albert. I had to patch up some details, including finding an apartment and giving some notice at my current job. The latter was not as easy as I had anticipated. Flo had taken me under her wing at the pharmacy, and she was devastated that I was going. She didn't really say this; I just realized it much later. Instead, she started treating me very badly. She was rude and abrupt and finally just asked me to leave before my time was even up. I cried for two days about this. I never wanted to hurt anyone, especially somebody who had been so good to me. I was shaken up. My first real career job, and I felt as if I'd been fired. Something still told me this was the right decision for me. I have completely forgiven Flo. She was a lonely lady who felt as if she was losing a daughter. I was a young girl ready to spread my wings.

I headed off to St. Albert with my mom to find an apartment. It had to be just the right type. I had high expectations with low pay at this age. I found a delightful, little Austrian-looking apartment near the edge of the city. It looked like it belonged at the bottom of a ski slope in the Swiss Alps. It had two bedrooms, a fair-sized kitchen, and a balcony, and the layout was very neat. The price was high for me at that time, and my mom tried to talk me out of it. I was convinced that this was the right place, and I signed the contract on my first rental space! Wow! Was I excited! How much better could life be? I'd be back with my friends, working a job that I would love, and in my first, cool apartment! I was suddenly on cloud nine and not at all blue or depressed. Life was turning around and on its way up.

During the next few months it was going *up*, but I didn't really see it or feel it. I was so busy at this store. We were doing prescriptions manually without a computer then, and there were many days that we filled more than two hundred prescriptions. I loved the pace and the learning. Making compounds of creams and powders mixed together by first calculating the measurements was incredible. I was finally doing what I had been trained to do. It was easy to make new friends at the store as I had been there the summer before. All was looking and feeling up.

At home, I was having fun in my apartment. I had to get used to being alone. My friends came over from time to time, but they were incredibly busy at university in their second year. I didn't buy very many healthy groceries. I was alone and ate whatever I wanted on most days. Sometimes I had popcorn, cookies, or ice cream for supper. I knew better, but at the time it seemed less expensive and definitely easier than cooking a meal for one person.

The news spread about my having my own apartment. Most friends were still living at home and had university on their minds. It was cool to know of someone having her own place. Therefore, my pad became quite a party place. It was contained mainly to weekends but had many late nights and a few new "friends." My old school friends didn't come by as much as they had the university crowd to party with. Things were not exactly as I had expected, but all seemed really good.

As time went by, I became lonelier, and my friend Joan gave me a kitten to help me feel better. It was so cute. I named it K. C., for kitty cat. Also at the time, I was infatuated with a boy named Casey. Budgeting was also getting a little difficult as I was living beyond my means in that apartment. I decided to get a part-time job at Dairy Queen to supplement my wages. I had worked there as a teenager, and they were happy to hire me back. I worked one weeknight and a shift on the weekend. It kept me busy, helped me make more friends, and helped a bit financially.

Life was good, and I went on a trip to see my auntie Marilyn and my grandparents in Arizona. My friend Greg took me to the Edmonton International and then picked me up. He is an old boyfriend and a wonderful guy! The trip wasn't very expensive as I had a place to stay in Mesa at a trailer resort with my grand-parents. Looking back on my life, I can honestly say that by the time I got to Arizona, I was on a very big high, though I wouldn't have recognized it then. I met another young girl at the pool, and we decided we needed to party lots. She was from the area and knew of a few "after hours" bars where people younger than twenty-one could come to dance once the bars stopped serving alcohol. We decided to drink first. The bar was very cool and very busy.

My friend went off on her own, and I found a place to sit near the dance floor. I noticed a guy looking at me so I looked over and smiled. He was gorgeous! He came over, asked me to dance, and told me his name was Lynn, and so began a new love affair! I remember thinking, *How can anyone be so cute, sexy and cool, all at the same time?* We had a blast dancing and talking. Soon he and his friends were asking us if we wanted to head to another party. Michelle and I decided there was no harm in that so we followed them. When we got to her car, we discovered that her vehicle had been broken into and my purse had been stolen! If my head was balanced, this definitely would have been a sign to head home. Here I was away from my country with no money or ID! My friend got sick in the bushes and then, despite all that … we headed to another party.

At the party, they got out some cocaine. I wanted *no* part of that and said I wanted to go. My friend went home and I went home with Lynn. Looking back, of course, I see how impulsive and insane I was. At the time, being in such a high (manic), I saw no harm—only fun! I was elated, free, feeling amazing, and with a gorgeous guy too! He had his own place. It was so cool. I hadn't met a guy with his own place before. We got to his apartment, and I jumped right into his arms with my legs wrapped around him. We had an exciting night.. I was falling in love! I'm lucky to have survived that night. God had some angels watching over me.

Lynn really treated me like a princess during that trip. He took me for walks in the park, out for dinner, and was amazingly kind. I entirely ignored my family once I found Lynn. When a person is in a high, she usually isn't very thoughtful or nice. My family helped me with some money. I am sure my grandparents weren't impressed with my gallivanting with a strange man in a strange country, but they kept their thoughts to themselves. I was really scaring them during my stay. The thing I hate most in life is hurting others, yet I know I have done this many times. As I forgive others, I pray that others will forgive me.

Well, needless to say, I didn't sleep much during this holiday, and soon it was time to head back to Edmonton. I said my tearful good-byes to Lynn. We promised to keep in touch, and he said he would love to move to Canada one day. I somehow got back on the plane without ID (security has greatly improved since then). I was sad but still flying high (not just in the plane either!) My brain was on a chemically imbalanced high. I was sleepless, overly confident, and feeling too great!

I returned to my jobs and my life in St. Albert, newly in love. Lynn kept his promise and phoned me often. He enjoyed teasing me about the sport of curling. I was on a team, and he couldn't figure out why people would throw rocks down the ice and then sweep the rocks! It was really fun trying to explain the sport to him when he was living in a place where curling wasn't even heard of. We talked about him coming for a visit, and we even discussed a future. It was all so exciting and surreal. But soon, the "kite strings" were cut and my life took on a new direction.

Chapter 5
Dark Blue

O my soul, why be so gloomy and discouraged? Trust
in God!—Psalm 43:5 (*The Living Bible*)

As the "kite" slowly started to descend, I didn't notice too many changes in my life. Maybe I wanted to sleep a bit more, but I did need to catch up! I wasn't socializing at much as I once did. Soon, however, the kite crashed and I was lower than low. Noticeably in a deep depression, my life was drastically changing. What happened to the optimism? What happened to the quick, clear thinking? What happened to my need to constantly socialize and talk? What happened to my libido? What happened to my late, late nights with no need for sleep? I really don't think too many people at work noticed the change, as I kept my regular hours and just didn't talk a mile a minute!

At home, however, life was a different story. I became reclusive and subdued. I didn't talk to anyone but my mom over the phone and even then I mainly cried. My desire to go out with friends or have them over was nonexistent. I really started to hate myself and what I was becoming. While at home, I cried almost constantly. I would fall asleep crying, wake up crying, and jump in the shower anyway. My strong desire to fulfill my responsibilities kept me showing up at work. I think I even did a fairly good job. When I look back on this aspect of that depression, I am quite amazed that I was able to function in a work setting, when, really, I was truly falling apart inside.

I suppose work gave me a different level of concentration or distraction from my constant gloom. As I sank lower and lower, I refused to take any calls from Lynn. Eventually he stopped calling—another person I was responsible for hurting. To this day, I pray for Lynn and hope his life turned out better for not having me in it. Bipolar disorder, when not controlled, leaves a trail of mistakes and hurts. All one can do is to ask to be forgiven. Some things in life we cannot control, and this was one for me. I was barely surviving, and I couldn't have someone in this world thinking he loved me when I truly felt unlovable!

My family, and in particular my mom at this stage was my saving grace. God works through his angels in a special way. During one phone call with my mom, I was just a mess, and she knew I needed her in St. Albert. She left her job for a few days and drove a couple of hours north. As happy as I was to see my wonderful, loving, caring mother, I really don't think she was happy to see me in the state I was in.

I cried most of the time and was very anxious. Many tan- trums were thrown in front of her (children tend to show their *worst* behavior to their parents). I would pull my hair hard, yell, scream, and pound the floor with my fists. Depression can also bring about extreme anxiety, and this is the stage I was in. I remember wanting to beat the monster out of my body. I would say things like, "Go away! Get out of my body! I don't want you around." In retrospect, I was correct in feeling a monster was trying to take me over. I truly believe now it was Satan. He had found a messed up young girl with bipolar disorder to become his next victim. At the time, though, I only knew I felt completely horrible and hated being who I was. Thankfully, my mom loved me so much she was able to find the help we needed. I say "we" because this disorder certainly affects the whole family. Sometimes, I feel amazed that, after what I have put my family through, they even talk to me, let alone love me! A singing group called Farmer's Daughter sings a song called "Family Love," which is about this topic. One line says, "Family

love still believes when the whole world is pointing a finger."
This was my wonderful family described perfectly.

My mom heard through a friend about a gynecologist who
worked in St. Albert. She was thinking about my missed periods
and relating it to hormones, etc. as being the possible cause for
my gloom. We were able to get an appointment and went to
see this doctor. It took merely minutes for the gynecologist to
understand that I needed to be in a different doctor's office. Soon
we were recommended to a psychiatrist in Edmonton. This was
the beginning of some serious help my body, mind, and spirit
had been longing for. Although this move can be quite scary,
anyone unsure and confused about life should definitely seek
professional mental help.

My mom came with me to see the psychiatrist in Edmonton.
His name escapes me, but his expertise and diagnosis was important. I don't really remember what we talked about, but given
my history, he decided the symptoms I'd been displaying over
the past couple of years sounded like manic depression (which
is what they called bipolar disorder back then). He said Lithium
would probably be my best alternative to keep me from going
as high as a kite again. I didn't understand much of this, but I
knew I didn't want to remain feeling like this. I was in so much
emotional pain!

During this time, I remember thinking, *Wow, I must be very
messed up. I am seeing a psychiatrist! Only crazy people see psychiatrists!* And I was probably right. At the time, my thinking, my
chemicals, and all of my being *was* off track and crazy. Sometimes
we need redirection through God or God's helpers to get us back
into balance in life. This was certainly the case for me at this time.
At least this man had given me a diagnosis and some small ray
of light to grasp on to.

When I was back in Calgary, the other doctor had merely said
I would grow out of it and it was only an age thing! If only he
knew how far off his diagnosis was!

I went to the pharmacy (not the one where I worked) and filled my prescription for Lithium. I still remember the day so clearly. I was scared, embarrassed, unsure, and angry that I had to do this. Why did I have to go public and feel like I was declaring to everyone? "*I am crazy!*"

Somewhere deep down inside, though, I believed there was a bit of hope. I started on the Lithium right away. Within a few days, I was already feeling somewhat better. Within a month or so, I was back to my normal self (even though at the time it was hard to define my normal). I was more optimistic, much happier, and I began to socialize a bit more. Balance was happening in my chaotic up and down life!

My mom was very happy, as was the rest of my family. Mom had long since returned home to Calgary once she knew I was sane. Life in St. Albert carried on and things were good!

Three months later I had a follow-up appointment with the same psychiatrist in Edmonton. I remember the smile on my face and the light in my eyes as I told him how well I was doing and how great I was feeling. The doctor looked at me and said, "Well, if you are doing that well, you can go off your pills." This is a simple statement when first looked at, but one that in retrospect brings me to tears because it almost led to the end of my life.

I don't want to blame the doctor for deciding to tell me this, but I know at the time (1986), enough information was around about manic depression and Lithium for a regular doctor to know a person with this disorder does not just "go off" medication and stay sane. Lithium is a very different medication in that it is specified as an "anti-manic" agent, which means it works carefully on *not* allowing a person to get into the extreme highs. It doesn't really specifically deal with the depression part of the disorder, but it regulates depression by not allowing a person to get really high, therefore not allowing a person to get very low. I've come to realize that it is an amazing drug for me and for many people out there with bipolar disorder if it is used properly. I have forgiven the doctor.

Chapter 6
Madness

See my sorrows; feel my pain; forgive my sins.—Psalm 25:18 (*The Living Bible*)

I continued to feel quite good, and then better, and then amazing! I, of course, was feeling too good but not realizing it. I began to hang out with a younger crowd as my friends were really busy with university and working. On the weekends I would go to parties, hang out at the bars, or have people over. It is interesting to me that when I was feeling depressed, I always knew something was wrong, but manic highs can really sneak up on a person and you often don't even realize what is going on. During this fun, feel-good time, my sister Tracey asked me if she could move in with me as she wanted to go to the University of Alberta in Edmonton. I said that would be great and she moved back up north with me. We both realized that my current apartment was too expensive so I searched for a more reasonably priced one. I moved into Alpine Place, thanks to my brother-in-law, Ken's, help (again), for about one hundred dollars a month cheaper. My little sister moved in soon after. It was so nice to have family close by.

I hadn't realized how much I missed Tracey. She became busy with university courses and working at Smittys pancake house. I remained busy with my two jobs and my social life. I was becoming full of energy, life, and talking! All of my senses were so very "aware", and I really didn't need much sleep. These are all typical signs of a manic high. Tracey and I were getting along pretty well, other than my obsessive need for order and her more laidback attitude about our apartment. Around this time I started to see a guy named Marlon. He was dark, very cute, mysterious, sexy, and dangerous! What a great combination when a person is in the midst of a high! I became obsessed with Marlon, and I think he became a bit obsessed with me. Well, here I was, an older woman with a place of her own. I was full of spit and vinegar, pretty enough, loved to talk and party, and very willing to make him happy. What normal nineteen-year-old male wouldn't become obsessed with this? I really don't think we felt anything more than obsession for one another, and this can become dangerous. The relationship was shallow on one hand but quite complex in another way. I was getting my way in that I could act like all guys (so I thought at the time) and just not get involved emotionally. No strings, right? Whenever we are involved in someone else's life, God decides which strings remain intact. Marlon would show up after partying and being with his friends some nights. I was fine with that. We would also go to the bar together, and I would manage to make him jealous. Somehow we would still end up together.

Another sign of this disorder when one is in a high is extreme impulsiveness in one or all of the following areas: compulsive shopping, drinking, gambling, or promiscuity.

Tracey's perspective was one of caution. She saw the way Marlon was and that he wasn't a good choice for me. However, looking back, I know I wasn't a good choice for him either. In some weird "Bonnie and Clyde" way, we met each others' needs. There was something dark about Marlon at the time. I was so mixed up and ascending higher and higher that I only saw this as exciting! One night I was out with friends when Marlon showed up at our apartment. Apparently, he made the moves on Tracey. Tracey reluctantly told me about this one evening. She was hoping that finally I would see the light. I have to admit that I was a bit upset with him, but not too much. From Marlon, it was almost expected. Much to Tracey's chagrin, I continued the relationship anyway.

The upward spiral continued. I was involved in many things at our Shoppers Drug Mart. We were an incredibly busy store. The mall was organizing a float for the Rainmaker Rodeo parade. I got involved in that too. They hosted an air band competition in the mall around that time, and of course I entered that with a friend. I had no fear. It felt like I was on top of the world, and I was loving it! I was only getting about two to four hours of sleep at night at this time. I wasn't tired either—again, a sign of a manic high. Energy and ideas were clear and abundant. Life was good, and I could handle anything! Unfortunately, people around me didn't feel the same way. I was difficult to be around. To others, I was annoying, bossy, obsessive, crazed, and talked way too much!

I finally came to my senses and broke up with Marlon. But how do you really break up with a guy you didn't have a true relationship with anyway? I tried and neither of us seemed too upset.

One night I ended up at a party with and older group. They were around Roni's age and some of them knew her from her high school years! This was really exciting for me because Roni was a hero in my mind, and I had dealt with a bit of an identity crisis through my later teen years and early twenties. I really wanted to be like her. She was cool, street smart, and fun. She was strong and independent. Roni had so much going for her. She loved to party! Roni really did have so many awesome God-given talents and abilities. I was and am a lot different from her, yet I was trying at times to live a life like hers. Add this to a manic mess and you have a mixed-up recipe!

I met a really cool and awesome guy at this party. His name was Kale. He was calm, cute, and kind. Does this sound a bit different from Marlon? He really was almost the opposite of Marlon. Even in my mania, I saw this guy was really a godsend. We started to date in a traditional way. We talked (which I was extremely good at, at the time!), made meals together, sat by the fire, and even partied a bit. Even writing these words makes me feel calmer. I believe he was sent to calm me and help me. Unfortunately, I was so out of control at this time that Kale alone couldn't fix me.

Sleep was almost nonexistent for me now, and I spent many waking hours thinking, imagining, and seeing some things I really didn't want to see. I began to predict things would happen, and then they would happen. I remember sitting up with Tracey late one evening. She'd joined me after she'd gone to a party or work. We were talking, and I told her there was going to be a very big storm that night. At the time the sky looked fine, and she couldn't understand me. I believe she was getting used to this! Later in the night we had the biggest thunderstorm I ever remembered in St. Albert. Tears fell down my face as I think I finally knew something wasn't right with me. I was out of my mind in some ways.

Rainmaker Rodeo was fast approaching as was the May long weekend. Tracey made plans to go out to the lake for the long weekend to meet up with my mom and dad. I had to work late on the Friday, so I had different plans.

Before I go further, I must give some background information on my pharmacy technician job at Shoppers and on a particular pharmacist that I was working with. Kate was a new graduate, and she'd been hired after I'd been at the Shoppers Drug Mart for some time. She was friendly and thorough with the customers. We had an incredibly busy store. She didn't like me very much from the start (and that was before my high). Kate, I believe, felt intimidated a bit by me as I had a lot of practical knowledge about the job and she had a lot of book smarts. Because we were so busy we needed to work as a team, but she was often mad at me about one thing or another. I worked fairly independently and once a prescription was done, she had to sign it. Kate had two sisters she was very close to. She talked about them all the time. They came into the store to visit her often. Kate really loved her sisters, and they were very close. She did everything for them. I tried my hardest to get along with Kate, but she felt that I didn't treat her like my boss.

On this Friday of the May long weekend, I was working the twelve to eight p.m. shift. Around 7:15 I got a call from my sister Tracey stating that her truck, "Theo," had broken down on the highway on her way to Pigeon Lake. I don't recall how she called me as it was before cell phones, but I remember being very worried about her being all alone stranded out on the highway. I went directly to Kate and gave her a great opportunity to make an "executive" decision as I asked her if I could leave forty-five minutes early from my shift to go and help my sister. It was a Friday before a long weekend, and we weren't even busy for a change. Kate said, *"No!"* Something to the effect of, "This is something Harvey would have to decide." That irritated me even more as just the week before, she was complaining that I had to treat her like a boss about some issue. Now I needed her help and her decision as a boss—a woman who had two sisters she would roll over backward for—to help me and she wouldn't. We argued and finally I left anyway. I have never to this day regretted leaving to help Tracey. I am sure that any decent human being would have done the same. Looking back, I know I wasn't completely healthy, and as I was escalating higher and higher, my mind wasn't always reasonable. But on this particular occasion, I felt I did the right thing.

God works in mysterious and sometimes hurtful ways. I lost my job when I returned to work on Tuesday. I wasn't completely surprised. Harvey didn't want to fire me, but it was me or a pharmacist, and he needed Kate more than he needed me. It hurt me a great deal as I had never been fired before. As devastated as I felt, I was quite calm about it. This was the part that worried my family the most, I believe. *Why would Shelley be so calm about this? What will she do now?*

God had a plan, and it went something like this: sleeping very little at all and running on fumes, I decided in a few days to pack a few things and head home to Calgary for a while. (I say "I" with hesitation as I truly believe God drove me there.)

By this time in my condition, I was truly hearing music talking directly to me. The songs had so much to say about my life. They were very explicit in lyric and meaning to my life. In particularly, the Bangles and Waylon Jennings for some odd reason were telling me many things. The one song by the Bangles told me to leave a letter at my friend Molly's house, so I did before I left. I have no idea what I said in the letter, but probably I was apologizing or something. In everything in life, one must find some humor. As Waylon Jennings belted out of my cassette player to the tune of "Luckenbach, Texas," and "Amanda," my mind decided that my *dad* was actually Waylon Jennings! It wasn't a question but a statement that I finally realized! Stupid me! Why had it taken so long to understand? I mean my dad loved country music. He was dark and handsome. He liked to sing. Dad was often away on business trips. It all just made so much sense (at least to a crazed mind it did). By the way, even though my dad likes to sing, he would be the first to admit that he's not very blessed in the vocal area!

During my three-hour journey to Calgary, I obsessively played only the Bangles and Waylon Jennings's Greatest Hits. I was on a mission, and my life was slowly coming to make sense through these songs, so I thought at the time. It is really quite astonishing to me to recall how "out of my mind" and mad I really was at this point, yet I had driven so far. God was certainly watching over me that day. When I finally arrived in Calgary I was a blithering idiot. My mom was quickly realizing that something was definitely wrong with me. I was behaving quite irrationally and talking a mile a minute. Many things I was saying were not making sense, especially the Waylon Jennings idea. Mom really wasn't sure what to do, but the next morning decided for us.

I barely slept, but when I finally did, I saw a bright light and angels calling me. It was profound. I woke up blabbering to my mom about some kind of new message I had dreamt about. Mom soon got up and made us some coffee. We were talking, or at least I was. My poor mother was inadvertently trying to reason with me and talk sense into me. I didn't know how she couldn't understand my perspective. This bothered me. My mom innocently went to pour me some coffee, and I suddenly "realized" (again, in my crazed mind) that she was trying to poison me! I started to panic. It all made sense. It all came together. She had started when I was younger but now was trying to finish off the job. She somehow made it seem so innocent, through sharing coffee. But I knew better. What was I going to do? My mom of all people was trying to kill me!

I was panicking, and suddenly the phone rang. It was my auntie Marilyn. Thank God! She would understand and help me. I went around the corner of the kitchen into the living room to share this terrifying news with her, but she didn't seem to understand or hear my urgency. Something had to be done soon. I was terrified of my own mother! So I did what any normal, rational, twenty-one-year-old girl would do. I grabbed my cowboy hat, my smokes, and my keys and ran for my car adorned in my short, red-and-white striped nightie imprinted with "Prisoner of Love." I honestly don't remember if I even put on shoes! I was a prisoner of my own mind running for my life! I got to my blue Super Beetle as fast as my legs could possibly take me. I've always been a fast sprinter, but as I got in and locked the doors, I was amazed and horrified to see my mom right at the passenger door trying to get in. Would she ever stop? I quickly put my key in the ignition and my foot on the clutch. Turning the key, I suddenly realized my car was dead. I looked at my mom as her eyes pierced deeply into my ignition, and I was sure she was somehow disabling my car. I thought, *How could this be? My mom? How could she hate me so? Why would she want to kill her own daughter?* Little did I know at the time, but what my thoughts were telling me were actually completely the opposite. I believe that through my mom's beautiful brown eyes, God performed another miracle in my life that day. Through my mom's honest and pure love for me, she disabled my car with God's help. I wouldn't have survived a car ride that day, and I might have hurt others as well. Thank you, God! (The very next day my car started on the first try ...)

Well, if at first you don't first succeed to escape ... try, try again! Out of the car I ran with my incredibly important personal belongings. I ran like the wind down the street away from my crazed mother. I'd never felt so afraid of anyone in my life. It should have been me who I was afraid of, but in this state of mind that was impossible to see. I ran and ran, not sure of where I was going at all.

My mom didn't follow. She went into the house, shaking uncontrollably. She knew she had to think clearly, so she called the police. They came quickly to take a report from her. She then called my dad and broke down crying. Suddenly, as I rounded the corner to a busier street, I saw a lady getting into a car. Really, she was a living angel to me that day. She asked if I was all right. I responded that my mom was chasing me and trying to kill me. One look at me must have said a thousand words to this lady, and she calmly asked if I would like a ride. I responded yes and asked her to please hurry. I jumped in and slouched down. Did I stop to think about where this kind lady might take me? No! I guess I didn't really care as long as I was away from my mom. This sweet angel took me over to a clinic in Midnapore. A few people asked me questions, and within an hour or two, my sister Roni and my dad soon arrived to talk to me.

As I relayed my horrifying discovery to them, they soon realized how crazed I was. They somehow privately determined that I profoundly needed help. Of course, in my ultimately confused mind, it was mom who needed the help. They made some quick decisions behind my back, and soon I was on my way to the Holy Cross Hospital in Calgary. Back in 1987 they had a psychiatric ward there, thank God. My dad and Roni took me in and somehow convinced me that this was where I needed to be. I have no idea why I didn't argue or even throw a tantrum about going into the hospital. I mean, I had never gone into the hospital before. They somehow convinced me that it was a good and safe place for me (possibly far away from my mom). Deep down inside I must have known I needed to be there.

I was calmly checked in and given a room. Dad and Roni were soon asked to leave, and I was on my own in a psych ward! I soon got my pajamas on (or was I still wearing them?), and a hospital robe, and my flip-flops (then known as thongs) and merrily went to the lounge area to meet some people. I've always been very social. Here I was, higher than any kite or jet and still wanting to talk. I felt, however, at this point that I had a higher calling. Now it was all making sense to me. This is what I thought: *Now I know why my dad and Roni brought me to this place. I am supposed to heal and help these poor people. Anyone can see they are troubled. The girl on the couch is extremely anorexic. They boy hunched in the chair is terribly depressed. The man over by the kitchen is talking to himself and must have schizophrenia. Ahh, so this is my purpose.* Robe, sandals, and all, I was feeling a little like Jesus! I felt elated and happy to help. Within minutes, I had an entire table full of new friends. I was somehow able to talk to them all at the same time!

There had to be seven or eight people around the table! I started handing out cookies and talking a mile a minute to these troubled people. The whole ward started to buzz, and I don't think the nurses liked it very much. The depressed man looked up and smiled. The anorexic girl actually took a bite out of her cookie! To my amazement she started to fill out in the face and put on weight, just after one bite! Of course this is what I wanted to see for this girl, and in my confused mind, it actually happened. It didn't take too long for the nurses to realize things were getting out of control, especially for me, the "healer." They wanted to escort me to my room. At first I was willing but then realized they had an ulterior motive. I saw a needle in one of the nurse's hands and I freaked out! They were trying to kill me too! I was so extremely paranoid at this point. I kicked and screamed and they called in more help. It turned out that this five foot, one hundred-ten pound girl had more strength than they ever would have imagined! It is amazing how strong a person can become when she feels threatened. I ended up kicking over a two hundred-pound nurse and probably hurt many others.

Finally they won the battle, and a needle full of Haldol began to do its trick. I was still scared and yelling but slowly calming down. They put me into my bed and my butt really hurt! Soon another image appeared in the middle of the room in the air. The Haldol was a tranquilizer that had me hallucinating about a Smurf-like baseball player doing tricks in the air. I recall giggling, and then I must have passed out cold.

I remained in the hospital for many days. At first I would only see Roni. I felt safe only with her in my paranoid mind. My poor mom was only staying sane by being given little tidbits of information that Roni would pass on to her. Through medication and time, I was slowly descending and becoming less paranoid. I was now willing to see my dad and my auntie Marilyn. Mom took a bit longer, but while still in the hospital, I did see her along with the others. I very soon came to trust her again, but I am not so sure I can say the same about her trusting me. Lord, what I put her through! What I put them all through! It wasn't pretty, and I am eternally grateful for a beautiful, forgiving family and a forgiving God.

Within a week or so, a group of specialists decided I was well enough to go home. Thankfully, I had a place to go to. Without my parents' unconditional love, support, and home, I wouldn't have been ready in the least! Along with antipsychotics, antidepressants, Lithium, and love, I was sent home with my parents.

Poor Kale heard through the grapevine of my breakdown, and he came willingly to see me. In retrospect, if I could have warned people off having a relationship with me, I would have certainly done this for Kale. Here was a guy in his mid-twenties looking for someone special to begin a life-long relationship with and he ended up with a nut! I was lucky to have a guy like him at that time in my life, but I don't think he was! He offered to take me back to St. Albert to pick up a few of my belongings. I wouldn't completely move back to Calgary as my sister Tracey was still living in my apartment. So, St. Kale drove me in his van all the way to St. Albert and back to Calgary (about three hours away) to collect some of my clothes and belongings. He was so kind. I believe he knew instinctively that our relationship was over, but he didn't seem to care. He just wanted to do what he felt was right—a real knight in shining armor. Girls don't come across true gentlemen much anymore. Thank you from the bottom of my heart, Kale! How I pray that your life has turned out happy and fulfilled with love from someone as true and noble as you.

Kale was right. Our relationship had come to an abrupt halt due to my mental condition. I really couldn't take care of myself, let alone a relationship with someone else. The medication I was on left me feeling quite dopey and disoriented a lot of the time. It was working, however, as I was back to almost "normal" when looking at highs and lows. It was, however, a drug-induced normal and inside I was fairly messed up. As the descent continued, I began reflecting on my young adult life. The thoughts weren't so nice! Most of you have heard of negative self-talk. Well, I began to learn this very well. I was becoming the queen of putting myself down and thinking only of the negative things of my most recent past. God most certainly wasn't part of my thinking or I may have considered his ultimate forgiveness. Instead, the Devil took over my thoughts and my life over the next few months.

I had started seeing a psychiatrist at this time. It was a fairly good relationship for me as he knew a great deal of information about manic depression (bipolar disorder), and my parents learned a lot from him. Also, believe it or not, I was all talked out for now and he loved to talk. He talked for 90 percent of the time we met. I didn't think that was how psychiatrists worked, but it was working for me at the time. As I continued to descend past "normal," I wasn't in the mood to share many things from my horrible past with anyone. The doctor monitored my medications and told my parents how important it was for me to *stay on my Lithium*. I was also on a strong antidepressant called Tofranil. These were the only two medications I recall being on at this time. He reinforced that Lithium was the only anti-manic agent out there (at the time), and it worked quite mysteriously as it doesn't allow people to go into a high. Again, Lithium doesn't really work on the lows other than not allowing the roller-coaster effect to begin. If a person doesn't get high, he or she won't get low. This is truly the way the medication works.

Right around the end of this manic high, my grandmother got sick. At first they diagnosed Grandma Rhyason with a blood clot in her leg. I recall seeing her in the hospital when I was flying high and having a very long and deep discussion about life. She was in a white gown, and I felt that she looked like an angel. I was not concerned about her as the doctors gave her a good diagnosis. A few days later, my immediate family had a night out at a restaurant and Tracey was visiting too. I was still on my high as I remember it to be a happy night. Feeling content to have all of the Wards together again, I didn't have a clue mom and dad had an ulterior motive in having us meet. Near the end of the meal, my mom said Grandma had been diagnosed with pancreatic cancer. She said she would only have about two months left to live! We were in shock. Grandma was a vibrant, happy, healthy, giving, kind, and beautiful lady. How could this be? Was it really true? She was only in the hospital for a minor clot that they had already taken care of. All of us kids started crying in disbelief and horror.

Unfortunately, the doctors were right, and my grandma started a rapid decline in her health. Very soon, she was only drinking Ensure for her meals. She had always been a healthy, happy, lovely woman and now she looked so ill. How did this happen? Why did this happen?

These were my ongoing questions as I saw my grandma grow weaker and sicker over the next couple of months. Along with her debilitating health came my declining mental health. At this unstable point in my life, hearing that a lady such as this was so ill was hard to take. My grandma and I were quite close, and I respected and loved her very much. My poor mom! She had a terminally ill mother and a depressed daughter to deal with all at once. It was a difficult time in both my parents' lives. Somehow, God gives us strength to get through the toughest times.

Very soon, news came that my grandma had passed away. The news struck me like a bullet in the heart. I had never lost anybody close to me, and I wasn't in the best shape to be dealing with death. A beautiful lady who had so much to give had been taken away. Why? And most importantly, *why not me?* I had so little to give this world. I was boring, sick, horrible, and down. Really, I had so little to offer this world compared to my wonderful grandma. I was really angry at God at this point, although at the time I am not so sure God even entered my mind much. It is sad to admit because this was when I needed him more than ever.

Chapter 7
The Color Black

When you go through deep waters and great trouble, I will be with you. When you go through rivers of difficulty, you will not drown! When you walk through the fire of oppression, you will not be burned up—the flames will not consume you. For I am the Lord your God, your Savior.—Isaiah 43:2–3 (*The Living Bible*)

Lithium had become an integral part of my life and sanity. However, at the point in my life after the hospitalization and the crazy, extreme high that I had been on, the damage of that particular high had already been done. The law of gravity states that what goes up must come down. I am living proof of that! I had gone as high as possible, and now I was beginning my lowest descent ever. I became less and less talkative and more and more self-defeating. When I would talk, it was about how horrible, stupid, and awful I was.

My family tried so hard to help me see the light, and again my dad had a couple of really deep conversations with me at this devastatingly low time in my life. It felt at the time that the walls of depression were impenetrable no matter what kind words and thoughts were passed my way—they merely bounced right off me. I was a hopelessly sinking boat, and I refused to grab any life preservers thrown my way.

Again I must switch to present day. I am in the Dominican Republic with my husband. I am sitting on my balcony listening to the pouring rain, falling in beat to the Dominican music playing in the background. A band not far away is playing beautiful domestic music. We have had nothing but rain since we arrived on Wednesday (two days ago). It is uncommon, but tropical storm Bonnie is upon us. God is all about his own timing. My husband and I are true sun worshippers, thus coming to a tropical place such as this during our own summer. However, the rain is nice, and it gives me a chance to concentrate on writing. My kids are safe and sound at home in Lac La Biche with my parents. Thank God for wonderful grandparents! We are here to relax and enjoy the perfect beauty of the Caribbean for two whole weeks! We are truly blessed and thankful! Not many people from Alberta come to the Dominican Republic in the summer. It seems that most Albertans save this type of vacation for the long, cold winter.

Also related to God's timing and extreme, wonderful "coincidence" is a small story of what happened to Dale and me tonight at our resort. We had just finished dinner and were deciding to go outside to listen to the entertainment. When we left the restaurant, we realized it was raining again and the outside entertainment had been cancelled. Dale asked if I would like to go see the end of the children's show. I thought we might as well as at least it was a covered venue. We headed over to the theater, and just as we were arriving, people were leaving. The show was over! We decided to walk over to the area near the empty bar and open air. Almost everyone was gone when suddenly I heard a song playing on the music system. It was the song from our first dance at our wedding, "I Swear" by John Michael Montgomery. I couldn't believe it! We danced the whole song together, and I felt the experience was amazing. I really don't think I heard another country song in the Dominican Republic before or after that song. Something brought us directly to that spot that night, halfway across the world to hear our song played just for us! It was very rejuvenating, spiritual, and wonderful.

My depression was feeling very long and cold. Longer than any depression I had experienced, I could feel no sun or warmth. I shut out most people from my life and talked only if talked to. I was not such a nice person to be around. All that I truly wanted to do was sleep and sleep and sleep. At least with sleep I could temporarily escape from myself. My family would not let me, of course, and tried many things to cheer me up. Unfortunately, when a person feels like this, often the effort of others somehow makes one feel even worse. The only thing that kept running through my mind was, *Everyone is trying so hard, and all I can do is sleep and complain in my head. Why am I such an awful person?* Now I know that I was depressed and very sick. It is hard to rationalize anything when you are in such a state. *Everything* in life is out of perspective. It certainly didn't feel as if anything was about to change or get better. Life seemed impossible, and I felt unworthy of happiness at this point.

(A song just played at the festival night close by and is appropriate for this portion of my story. The rock group Queen had many awesome songs, but a signature song of theirs, called "Bohemian Rhapsody," just played. In this song is a line that says, "I sometimes wish I'd never been born at all!" At this dark, dark time in my life, this is exactly what I felt like.)

My grandma had died, and I had no close friends in my life as I hadn't allowed anybody in for months. My family put up with me very kindly, but they were family, right? I had no job and was living with my parents. Just existing felt painful. Depression hurts deeply. "Hopelessness" was a synonym for Shelley.

One early Monday morning in August, I woke up very much the same as other days. My family had gone to work, and I had slept in somewhat. I put on some old gray sweats and a striped T-shirt, ready to start my miserable day. My head was different, but it is hard to explain. My dad came home for lunch and I made him some kind of food. He was happy to see me doing something, anything at all other than sleeping. After lunch, he gave me a kiss and a hug and headed back to work. I cleaned up and went about my business.

About an hour later, I was lying on my mom and dad's bed, ready to die. I had taken many, many Tofranil tablets. Somewhere in the darkness, something told me that life wasn't worth living anymore. There was too much sadness to bear, and I was hurting others too much to tolerate it anymore. I truly saw no alternative, although I really do not recall planning any type of suicide. It was almost like I was the recipient to *someone else's* plan. I had written a note to my parents and was waiting to die when I made a final phone call. I called Roni at work. I recall nothing about this phone call. God made it for me!

The following script was written by Roni:

Roni: Hi, Shelley. How are you?

Shelley: I'm good. (I lied.)

Roni: What are you doing?

Shelley: Just lying on mom and dad's bed. I just wanted to say I love you.

(Roni knew something was terribly wrong now.)

Roni: Did you take your medication today?

Shelley: Yes, all of it.

Roni: You took all of your pills?

Shelley: Yes, I took them all. I'm going to go to sleep now.

In a split second it all came together for Roni. She told me to get up and get some water. She asked me to drink a whole bunch of water and then to try to stick my fingers down my throat to make myself vomit. Roni told me she would be right there and to make sure the doors were unlocked. As Roni fled her work to frantically drive to Mom and Dad's house, she thanked God that her coworker knew of my situation with depression and was very helpful in contacting my parents.

Unfortunately, neither Mom nor Dad were available, so

messages were left that there was an emergency at home. Roni also gave her friend my parents' address and instructed her to call 911 immediately and she left on a rampage. This was a time before cell phones. Roni had lost all contact with me and knew she had to get to me fast! It took her fewer than ten minutes to travel quite a distance. When she arrived, the front door was still locked. She banged on the door to no answer. Roni doesn't recall how she got into the house but I believe God opened a window. The next thing she remembered was the paramedics taking over and asking her to move aside.

At that moment, Roni saw our dad standing behind her, and they clung to each other for dear life. She recalled the paramedics working on me on the gurney, but they weren't moving me anywhere. She thought this was odd. Roni wondered why they weren't quickly taking me into the ambulance and to the hospital. Time passed slowly when they finally moved me into the ambulance, but it again seemed an eternity to Dad and Roni until they finally took off. It was excruciating waiting for this to happen. They found out later that the paramedics actually lost me twice before transporting me to the hospital.

The next thing Roni recalls is being in the hospital and hearing from the doctor that the next few hours were critical. The pills I had taken had already absorbed into my system, so they didn't believe pumping my stomach would be effective. They were going to have to put me on a dialysis machine and if I made it through the night it would be extremely fortunate.

Wow! Roni thought. *How did we get here? What has happened to my sister? What are we going to do?*

There were so many questions and very little answers at that time. Soon a counselor took my dad and sister to the family room where my frantic mom joined them. The counselor was really helpful.

The prognosis was not great. The doctors told my parents that I not only took one of the strongest antidepressants, but I had taken a lot. If I did make it through, there would almost certainly be brain damage. My family was feeling very bleak, very dark, and not completely hopeful. They were feeling helpless and hopeless. *What had gone wrong? Why couldn't this young girl get better? Why was life such a difficult thing for her?*

My mom soon came back into my room and held on to my hand for dear life. She talked to me straight from her heart about hanging on and how much they all loved me. She talked to me about how I couldn't let go and how they all needed me. Mom prayed for me. My mother's fear was that as much as she was trying to show me love and purpose at this most critical time, I probably couldn't hear her—but God heard!

Even hopelessness is not too hard for God. He gave my family a ray of hope one morning when I suddenly opened my eyes, squirmed, and squawked through a very hoarse throat, "Hi. I need a cigarette and an chicken McMuffin!" This is what I asked for when I came out of the coma I had been in for days. Not surprisingly, it brought out tears of joy in my family. I was alive!

Depression and suicide are extremely difficult things to understand. I don't even know what to mention about signs to look for, in hopes of prevention of suicide. I really wish I had some amazing answer here, but I really think that an incredibly huge, impactful decision like trying to commit suicide, is very individual and personal. I truly believe that many people act as if things aren't much different than in the past few days. Signs of impending suicide often aren't apparent at all. Why would a person want to give away his or her deep, dark secret? What if he or she was stopped? In my case, I honestly think it was second-degree suicide attempt. I really don't recall *preplanning* anything. That particular morning, I believe I had just had enough of myself, and I couldn't take *me* like this any longer. I couldn't hurt others around me any longer. I am so very, very sorry for those of you who may have had to deal with a suicide in your family or a close friend. It is such an incredibly painful experience for those left behind. We all want answers, but sometimes they are so hard to find.

While writing this book I came across an article on the Internet, and I cried for a long time. Although I realize that many factors were involved in my decision to try to end my life, I understand now that this medication was more than likely a determining factor in my attempt. The article explained that it is apparent that Tofranil (the antidepressant I had been taking) can often be associated with suicide, especially in teens.

Be very careful with medication! There is always the balancing act of risk versus benefit when taking any medication. There are many options for people dealing with depression.

Chapter 8
Rainbow of Recovery

*For you are the fountain of life; our light is from
your light.*— Psalm 36:9 (*The Living Bible*)

My family was ecstatic and elated. I was confused. What had happened? Why was I in the hospital? *I had tried to do* what? I had so many questions and yet was still so foggy and confused. The doctors did some brain functioning tests on me, and amazingly, I had no apparent brain damage. What does a family do now? What was the next step?

Thankfully, God led us all to wonderful professionals whose expertise led me out of my hospital room and back to the Holy Cross, where I had been only months before, on my manic high. I had to go to recover; to get my medication in check; to get counseling; and to reconnect with life. Although my family was rejoicing, my dark mood hadn't just miraculously lifted. I was dealing with questions inside my head, such as, *Why did I do this? Why did they find me? Why did I have to live? Life is too painful for me. Look what I've done to my family!* This was a lot to bear. I had tried to kill myself! I was a mess, and even though I had been saved at this point in my recovery, I was far from grateful. Instead, I was miserable. I was far from being spiritually saved!

Needless to say, my parents truly acted as my guardians in this case and again booked me into the psychiatric ward at the Holy Cross. I didn't fight it. My fight was over. At the new hospital, they fed me well, and monitored my medication—which I believe was Lithium, an antidepressant, and something for anxiety.

The nurses were calm and kind. Many of the patients in the ward, including myself, went for daily walks with a nurse, and I received some counseling from my psychiatrist. I was eating well and several times my family came to visit me. Now I look back with tears in my eyes, and I say to my wonderful, kind, loving, and forgiving family, "Thank you for loving me, for visiting me with your busy schedules, and mostly for not giving up on me when I had totally and utterly given up on myself."

How many people have this kind of love in a family? I wish everyone had this type of family. I know I am truly blessed. Without them, my road to recovery would have been much, much longer or possibly nonexistent. Right around this time, my auntie Marilyn gave me a Bible. Thank you! A gift for *life*! She has always been such a special person in my life. The Bible she gave me was nice, but at the time I was completely ignorant of the effects and impact the words in these pages would eventually have on my life; I just needed time and other people to help me understand it.

If you are in the midst of helping somebody with this disorder, you will probably feel discouraged and frustrated many days, but please don't give up hope.

A kind, loving lady who never, ever gave up hope on me was my mom. She taught me how to knit, so I began knitting a sweater for my little nephew Trevor. Baking cookies in the hospital's kitchen was another activity I tried. These "normal" activities really were healing as it had been a long time in my recent high and extreme low that I had done anything quite like this. Somehow, I was contributing. I was able to give back to others in some small ways. Maybe I mattered. I slowly began to feel somewhat happier but still quite blue.

My mom and dad were told they could take me home very soon under one very important condition: I must attend *group* counseling daily. Now this did not thrill me. I was a fairly private person, especially when in a low. Why would I want to share any of my horrific life with strangers? How could they do this to me? Why did this have to be the condition? I promised to stay on my medication and to see my psychiatrist. Wasn't that enough? Apparently not. If I truly wanted to leave with my parents, I would have to sign up and promise to go to group therapy. At this point, I was sick of being in the hospital. They were good to me, but it was time to get out and be at home. It was a bit scary going home, but I felt I was ready to try. Reluctantly, I signed up for therapy.

The day finally arrived when Mom and Dad picked me up to go home. I don't really remember much about it. Group therapy would be at the hospital and start the following day. My mom realized there would be no way on earth that I could drive myself to downtown Calgary in my current condition. She decided to drive me and pick me up.

The very next day I faced one of my greatest fears and went to my first session. There were probably twelve or fifteen people sitting on chairs in a circle. The psychiatrist running the group was new to me. She introduced me and then barely said another word as people started talking randomly about their condition, situation, or fears. I was afraid they were going to put me on the spot, but they didn't. A young lady a few years older than me named Theresa shared. I remember thinking that she was neat, and I liked her honest and difficult story. Nobody cornered me that day, and the session wasn't quite as terrifying as I had imagined.

The next day was about the same. There was one important difference, though. I felt as a bear must feel after a long hibernation, once finally awakened by the warmth of the sun—a wonderful, beautiful, kind, smartly dressed lady named Shirley shared her horribly difficult story. I tuned in so very carefully, not letting anyone know of my interest. I believe this lady had something to do with my writing this book.

Shirley started her story off by remembering her past. She had this to tell: "A few years ago, I was so depressed I couldn't function as a parent. My husband had to do everything—cook, clean, take care of the kids. I couldn't possibly do these things as I was not able to even take care of myself. All I did was cry and sleep and cry and sleep. There was a time I didn't leave my bedroom for months other than to go to the bathroom. My husband brought me food. I didn't want anyone in my life. I didn't want to talk to anyone … I felt utterly hopeless!"

To some, her story may just sound very typical of someone in a deep depression. To me, at that particular time in my life, it was a true message of hope sent directly from God, I believe. I remember saying to myself, "Did I just hear what she said? *She has been depressed before?* This happy, healthy, funny, and kind lady had hit rock bottom too? How can this be? She appears totally put together. She is too 'with it' to have had anything in common at all with the likes of *me*!"

It was a connection of hope and truly what I needed at that particular time in my life. Shirley had something very much in common with me. She had also seen the darkness of depression, yet in a bit different way. Shirley had suffered many days as I had suffered. She had had no desire to go on in life. Shirley was now a happy, functioning lady! Could this possibly be? Could there really be hope for me? Yes, this "group therapy" had some purpose after all. I might have even smiled that day, but I certainly did not share!

As time went on and therapy did too, I felt less self-conscious and more comfortable. It was like a little family that I started caring about. Of course I wished I could help everyone, but thankfully, I knew this time I couldn't. I had to work on Shelley. And I did. Slowly, I started to believe I could possibly live a happy, normal life. Slowly, I started to let others in again.

Theresa from therapy and I had a couple of good conversations in the parking lot. She was a recovering alcoholic. She was a wonderful, kind lady. Although I didn't go to group therapy for very long, possibly three weeks to one month, the therapy had been extremely good for me. It was a stepping stone to readjusting and recreating the life I live today.

Over the next six months, I spent a lot of time at my mom and dad's house with them, my sisters, and my auntie Marilyn. They were the people I trusted and felt safe with. They are the ones who helped me slowly see the light in this world and who cared about me enough to keep believing in me on the scattered down days that were part of the recovery process. I was on my Lithium and antidepressants daily. Mom made sure to give me only a small amount at a time. Spending time at the health club helped me physically as it strengthened my body and spirit. The chemicals released when exercising are definitely healing to somebody in a depression. Exercising slowly helped to build me strong again. Still today, if I am having a bad time or day, I often go out for a brisk walk, even when the temperature is twenty below zero! Helping around the house and with some meals made me feel worthwhile in the home. I continued to knit, read, watch inspirational shows like *Oprah,* and spend time with my family. My relationship with my mom was somehow mended after my strange accusations of her and my attempted suicide. It is amazing to me what love and forgiveness can do. My mom and dad took me on a camping trip with their motor home about two months after my attempted suicide. It was lovely from what I see in the pictures, but I really don't remember much about the trip. The most important thing about that outing, however, was that I witnessed God's beauty in a new place. It was refreshing to experience a different setting. Traveling has always been important to me and my family. My parents travel a lot! This small trip did wonders for my soul and helped to solder some more pieces of me together.

Reading last night, I came across a sentence that really fits well in this part of my story: *When God forgives, he removes the sin and restores the soul.* Amazingly, God was healing me and showing forgiveness, and a reignition of my faith had begun, though it still had a very small pilot light. The strong faith I have for the Lord now was just beginning to be rekindled. Interestingly though, through events in my life, beautiful people who loved me, and choices I was making, God was definitely leading me closer to him. I just wasn't completely aware of it at the time.

Early in 1988 Calgary was preparing to host the Olympics. It was an exciting time to be in our city. My dad got a new job just as they were about to begin. This gave him a week off between jobs while the Olympics were on. He had some free time. Because I was still off too, we did a lot of things together. It was a beautiful time spent together and definitely part of my healing. We saw some curling, went down to Olympic Plaza a couple of times, and thoroughly enjoyed our time together. Reflecting on our relationship, I believe this was the first time I had spent that much quality time alone with my dad. It was the beginning of a much better, open, honest, fun, and active relationship. Since then, my dad and I have skied in the mountains together many times, gone horseback riding, golfed, and he has even been brave enough to go shopping with me a few times. Best of all, we have open communications, and I feel like my dad really loves me. He is an amazing, smart, fun, athletic, generous, good-looking man who I love very much.

If there is always a purpose in pain, maybe one of God's purposes was to bring my family closer together. We really became a stronger family unit through my illness.

I had been home from the hospital for about six months. I had been receiving unemployment insurance. Mom knew I needed a stepping stone back into the working world. Ironically, the volunteer job I was hired for was at the hospital that had saved my life. I began working in a gift shop at the Rockyview Hospital. I was really scared at first but soon realized that I could learn new things, serve customers, stock shelves, and work at the till. It gave me purpose and courage to believe that maybe I could work again one day. That day came sooner than I had imagined when I applied at the Shoppers Drug Mart close to Mom and Dad's house. I was hired very quickly and began a real full-time job with pay soon after. The new job was truly helping patch me up in so many ways. I was happy! I could work! I remembered most things about my pharmacy tech training! I was making new friends! I usually had a smile on my face! The world was looking up and Shelley Marie Ward was starting to feel human again!

Once again at present, I sit writing this book in the Dominican Republic at a beautiful resort. Whenever I've written during this amazing holiday, it has been in my room or on the balcony. I decided this morning to venture out to a new location by the coffee bar. I went for a little stroll, grabbed some strong coffee, and found a spot. The beautiful ladies working close by are just beginning their shift, and in the background I hear many of them quickly speaking Spanish amongst themselves. I have no idea what they are saying, but they often talk all at the same time and very quickly. I want to learn more Spanish soon. What a beautiful setting God has set me up in to complete my story! He has given me time and beauty to write my most difficult parts.

With so many positives in my life, my world was beginning to have many colors reappear and along with the colors, hope. God was healing me one stitch at a time. I met a close friend at Shoppers, and we started to do everything together. The onus on my parents had finally shifted.

One night, my friend and I went to a Billy Ray Cyrus concert. It was awesome! Afterward we decided to go to a bar for a while. While there, I looked over and saw a really cute young guy very close to me. I guess I was feeling more confident as I started talking to him, and we soon began to dance. His name was Bill. That night my life changed immeasurably.

We hit it off and started to fall in love. At that point, I would say Bill was my sun. He was bright and friendly like the sun, and he had, blond hair. Through his joyful, loving demeanor, I was able to witness many different shades of color I had never yet seen. Bill warmed my heart like sitting in a large ray of sun on the floor of a kitchen. As you recall, I had seen and dated many different people in my life. In fact, some weren't even mentioned! It was the path I had taken, and I cannot change that now. I had never truly fallen head over heels in love until this point. Talk about recovery for a broken life and heart. God had now given me this amazing love to help mend my torn-apart life. Lithium and love was definitely a super recipe in my healing!

Soon into our relationship, I told Bill about my bipolar disorder. He was young, innocent, and very accepting. Basically, I could write a book about Bill alone, but this is not my purpose. He was put into my life at a crucial time. I learned through this relationship that I was loveable and could love back. We traveled a lot together, made future plans, and saw one another as often as possible as he lived in Red Deer and I lived in Calgary.

A very odd coincidence occurred during our relationship. Bill and I had gone out to Jasper with a couple of friends skiing. While we were up in our second floor room playing cards, we looked down through the window and into the mezzanine, which had a bar. We saw someone with cowboy boots on, and he was sitting close to a girl. We were being silly and decided to make up a soap opera about what they were talking about, etc. They couldn't see us … until suddenly, the guy looked right up into our room—and you wouldn't believe who it was—Marlon! He definitely saw us as we quickly tried to retreat. Soon there was a knock on our door. It was Marlon and his girlfriend! Perfect! How do things like this happen to me? I had mentioned my past to Bill, but he knew of nobody specific. Marlon said he noticed some people from St. Albert and decided to come up. Bill, of course, invited them in for a drink. They declined his generous offer, thank goodness!

How could this guy so coincidentally show up in my life again? My life was finally getting good, and I didn't want him messing it up for me. Was Satan tempting me away from Bill? Thankfully, at this point in my life, there was no competition at all. It was a strange night!

As most long distance relationships become quite difficult, so did ours. Bill was two years younger than me and really wasn't ready to settle down and make a serious commitment. At that time in my life, I would have married him *yesterday*. Our relationship was beautiful and memorable but not meant to be. (Thank you, Bill, for the time we shared together. I wish you nothing but love, health, and happiness in your life today.)

Another exciting turn in my life around this time was that I joined a ladies' softball team! Tracey had moved back to Calgary into an apartment and acquired a great job at Nova Gas Transmissions. All us girls had played softball most of our lives yet never all three on the same team. Tracey and I joined Roni on a team called the Rebels. We had a lot of fun together on and off the field. The team was notorious for partying after games. I joined in on most days but really felt that this wasn't much for me. Intuitively, I must have known that partying wasn't on the "to-do list" for my recovery. Because people with bipolar have automatic highs and lows, they really don't need drugs or alcohol adding to the problem. Having a few drinks may feel really good at the time, but it is really a depressant. I had found that two or three days after too many drinks is when I would crash. Drugs work much the same with a temporary high interfering with a person trying to maintain balance.

Thankfully I was starting to put a few of these things together, and in the meantime, softball provided me with socialization, playing a sport, and meeting new people. I know the Rebels were also a portion of my healing, growing, and God leading me yet in a new direction. On our team was an amazing young girl named Liz. She was so pretty! She was so funny! She was so awesome at ball! Wow! Everybody loved Liz. I thought she was so cool! We seemed to have a lot in common. We both were blonde and close to the same age. We both loved ball. We both had the same middle name. We both weren't really into partying much. We both had a good sense of humor (I had found mine again!). We both had families with alcoholism. We both were deciding to go back to school. Ironically (or really just another of God's great plans), Liz and I talked one day on the ball field and realized we were registered in the same program at Mount Royal College! I had been considering a change for quite some time and had finally made the move to go back to school. Liz and I were both going into the education transfer program in the fall. We were also both terrified of going back to school, having been a bit older. Yes, Liz and I had a great deal in common and through ball and college, we soon built a bigger bond.

Before long, it was my twenty-sixth birthday, and I wanted to get some family and friends together to celebrate. My mom, dad, sisters, Auntie Marilyn, and my cousinRhea, and some friends met at the Ranchman's, a country bar with good music and dancing, in Calgary. Liz had invited a few of her own friends too.

The night progressed, and as I was opening a gift from my cousin, I looked over to see a young man staring at my new sweater and at me! He was very cute and had beautiful eyes and broad shoulders! I smiled, he smiled, and soon we were dancing. The young man ended up being Liz Thody's brother, Dale. Another piece of the puzzle was coming together. We quickly hit it off, danced the night away, and the rest is history. I had been in such a slump in my life with relationships before Dale. After Bill, really all of my friends were getting married, and I couldn't even find a close relationship. When I had started college, I decided to forget about men and just work hard and have fun with my friends. This decision eventually led me to Dale and our beautiful life together.

Though we had had our struggles in our relationship as

everyone does, it soon became apparent that we were destined to be together. Unfortunately, this didn't sit well with Liz. She really didn't like that her brother had fallen in love with her friend. I'm sure Liz had many reasons, but I really think that with her heart, she was merely afraid that one or the other would be badly hurt. Her brother had been previously married, and she saw the pain and anguish caused by deceit and divorce. Thankfully, Cindy, Dale's daughter, was a result of that marriage, and we are blessed to have her in our lives, though long distance. Liz and I became more distant as Dale and I became closer. I was really sad because I cared about Liz very much, but it was the way it had to be for a time. After about six months, I moved in with Dale, and we were soon engaged.

Soon after our engagement, I lost another beautiful lady in my life. My grandma Ward passed away at eighty-seven years old. She was a unique and strong lady who had lost her husband more than thirty years before. She taught me lots, and I miss her still. I was very sad about *this* grandma dying, of course, but my life didn't completely fall apart this time. My family was concerned about my reaction, naturally, but I was in such a different state this time. I was in control. I had my medication, love, and hope in my life.

Soon wedding plans were in progress! Yes, Shelley Marie Ward was getting married! I really couldn't believe it. My life was coming together. I was almost done with my third year in education and was engaged to a man I truly loved! Was this really my life? As I looked back, I could hardly believe my blessings. My friends had been married, and I had stood up as maid of honor at both my sisters' weddings. Was it really my turn?

On August 13, 1994, Dale and I were married in a beautiful church off Bow Trail in Calgary. The weather was absolutely gorgeous! I really felt like a beautiful princess on that special, special day. My sisters stood up for me and Liz stood up for Dale along with his friend Ned. Liz wore a tux and looked just as beautiful as my sisters did! My mom and dad walked me down the aisle. This was so special to me. I felt like I was *finally* giving back some happiness to them. What a marvelous, memorable day!

The colors of the rainbow were most definitely radiating down on my life!

Chapter 9
My Colorful Life

Now I can relax. For the Lord has done this wonderful miracle for me. He has saved me from death, my eyes from tears, my feet from stumbling. I shall live! Yes in his presence—here on earth!—Psalm 116:7–9 (*The Living Bible*)

From complete devastating darkness to the multiple colors of hope, my life had truly been transforming. God had a plan, and in his plan was my healing, growing, and learning to live with this difficult, unpredictable disorder. I completed university and put out my resume all over Alberta. My opportunities in finding a job in the city were almost nonexistent. This was okay with me as I realized that a smaller setting was exactly what I was looking for. I craved peace, no traffic, and a small town to live in. This is exactly what I received, minus the peace some days (I am a grade one teacher)!

On August 28, 1995, I was still working at a Shoppers Drug Mart in the pharmacy when I received a phone call from a principal in Lac La Biche. "We'd like to offer you a contract to work in a grade four position."

I was so excited! I accepted, of course. I was hired on my grandma Rhyason's birthday! She had also been a teacher—another angel watching over me. I headed to Lac La Biche, and Dale came to help me get set up. He stayed working in Calgary for a year as we were unsure about job security at this point. We commuted back and forth. My year was challenging and interesting. Thankfully, our old St. Albert neighbors the Moores lived in

Skeleton Lake only forty minutes from Lac La Biche. They have been like second parents to me, and I am blessed to have them in my life. It was so nice to know they were so close when my family was so far away. After three weeks at my job and having moved my world up north, six hours from Calgary and all of my family, I was laid off due to budget cuts. All of the schools in our area had to get rid of a new teacher. I was the newest teacher at this school. Although I felt devastated, I was far from defeated. I certainly wasn't ready to head back to Calgary where I knew there were no jobs. Instead, I substitute taught, and another job suddenly emerged in a high school in town. I would be teaching a special needs class. Even though I didn't feel completely prepared to teach such a course, they were in a tough situation and so was I! It is amazing to me that when a person has been through a lot of hard things, how much easier other challenges become. This was *nothing* as hard as dealing with my most serious ups and downs in life. This was not even close to as difficult. God would help me with this new assignment, and he did. I learned so very much from this teaching position at the high school, and it helped me attain a permanent teaching position in the division that first year.

At the beginning of the book I described how the last thing I wanted to be was a teacher. I truly felt that way at the time. However, God has his own plans, and I had had an interesting teaching experience during my pharmacy technician days at Shoppers' Drug Mart. I started an "adopt-a-school" program in which we invited a grade two class to visit our store. I proceeded to show them all the different parts of our store. We ended up in the pharmacy, and I taught them about what pharmacists and technicians do and how to be very careful about medication that may look very similar to candy. They saw a short video—and of course had a snack. It was short. It was sweet. And I loved it! Maybe teaching wouldn't be so bad after all! This is truly when my mind-set changed about becoming a teacher. Very soon after, I was registered at Mount Royal College in education.

Soon, Dale arrived in Lac La Biche and we began a search for our first home. It seemed surreal to me to be looking for a house. I had no clue about these things, but Dale did. He had already been independent and had lived in two different houses in his previous marriage. We didn't look at many places as the very first place we looked at, we loved! It was a beautiful, smaller, colorful home with an A-frame and a gorgeous loft. The cupboards in the kitchen were burgundy. There was sponge painting everywhere. Talk about my colorful life! I'm sure you've heard the saying, "God can dream bigger than us." This is exactly what happened with this home. I had always loved lofts and when I was a little girl I dreamt of a home with a loft in it after having stayed in Jasper with my parents at The Jasper Inn (which had a loft). I had long since forgotten this dream, yet here it was completed through the love of God. We had a gorgeous yard with a creek running through our property. Honestly, I thought I was dreaming.

This was a perfect setting for my little angel, who entered this world almost a year later. On August 15, 1997, our first little girl was born. Jamilyn Marie Thody was born on my mom's birthday, with only twenty minutes to spare. God's timing is amazing! I felt that somehow, a tiny bit of the pain I'd put my mom through years ago maybe healed a bit that day with this beautiful gift from God. I also felt God's true forgiveness of me. He must have loved and forgiven me fully to have given me such a perfect little gift! Jamilyn cried out like a lamb the night she was born.

Before long, I made a career choice to work with the *little* ones. I was hired for a grade two position at the elementary school. We soon had our next little blessing, Kristy Danielle Thody. She was so beautiful and precious. My little three year old, Jamilyn, said it perfectly when holding her in the hospital the day she was born, "Mom, I'm falling in love with holding her."

What a special time in a person's life! I was fortunate to go back to work part time after a year's maternity leave with Kristy. I was a busy, happy, healthy mom. Dale changed jobs about then too. He was able to walk to and from work in five minutes. God was certainly looking out for us. I had been mentally healthy and happy for about thirteen years at this point.

I feel that this is a good time to mention my experience with pregnancy and bipolar disorder. Up until my pregnancies, I was still being balanced by only Lithium and a multivitamin called Stressease. Once I discovered I was pregnant, I quickly went off my medication and replaced them with Materna, a maternal vitamin. The doctors know that taking Lithium during pregnancy can be dangerous to the fetus. I don't recall what type of problem can occur, I just know that I wasn't taking any risks with drugs or alcohol (I see horrible examples of the results of alcohol and drug use during pregnancy daily when teaching). Was I scared? Yes! I was terrified! When I became pregnant with Jamilyn, I had been healthy and balanced for nine full years. It was so terrifying to give up this control to God. I was pregnant, and I didn't want to change that. I had always dreamed of having a family but I really didn't see it happening during various times in my life. I had given up the dream when I had let God out of my life. Also, when in extreme highs and lows, I felt I could barely manage myself—how in the world could I become a mom? How could having children be possible for me? God can make it possible—and he did for me. Not only did I go off my medications during my pregnancies, I felt really good. In fact, talking to many other women about pregnancy and postpartum depression, I think I did very well. Hormones from pregnancy somehow kicked in for me, and I was able to cope amazingly well. That being said,

I do recall a few blue days during my pregnancies, but nothing significant.

After my pregnancies, I even nursed for four to six months. The hormones were still strong, and nursing was something I really believed in. I felt fortunate. However, around this four-to–six-month range, I began feeling some signs that were telling me I needed to be back on my medication. I experienced a bit more anxiety, was not sleeping very well, and was feeling blue. This is when I decided to wean, which wasn't very hard as I had introduced the bottle with my babies early on. Life is about balance, and my children needed a healthy mom! I slowly reintroduced Lithium into my life until the appropriate amount necessary for me was reached.

Dale and I were happy with our careers and our lives. We missed our family down south but immensely looked forward to every visit! Here we were, living in a beautiful small town with a perfect little family of two precious girls, and loving our jobs. We were so blessed!

This is when we made the decision to do something more permanent with our birth control. We decided Dale would get a vasectomy. He went in for the procedure without too much difficulty or pain, thankfully. Dale was a trooper! The doctors recommend that soon after, a guy gets checked for any remaining sperm. Dale did this too. Our doctor soon called us back to say he felt Dale should get one more operation done as the sperm count was low but still there. Reluctantly, Dale prepped for yet another day procedure in a very tender spot! I had dropped him off at the hospital this time and went home to be with the girls. A short time later, I received a call to pick Dale up. The doctor had decided against this second operation after all! He had called a urologist in the city to confirm that this second operation was unnecessary. The doctor in the city had said to him, "Don't worry if there is such a little sperm count. Pregnancy would be virtually impossible with such a low count."

Therefore, our doctor sent Dale home with me. He was still groggy from the medication.

Meanwhile, Dale's daughter, Cindy, came for her yearly visit from Texas for a few weeks in July. We always looked forward to her visits. Jamilyn loved to spend time with her big sister! This time, Cindy would meet Kristy for the first time as Kristy was now two months old. It was always an exciting time to have Cindy come to visit, but this time proved to be more exciting than usual. Cindy had a deep discussion with Dale and said she didn't want to go home. Her mom was and is emotionally unstable. She would drink a lot and had been abusive to Cindy around that time. Cindy was fourteen years old. I had predicted that she may want to come and live with us around this age. Under the circumstances, we were more than willing to help Cindy and have her live with us in Lac La Biche.

However, having a newborn and a very resistant ex-wife, Barb, to juggle wasn't going to be easy. We were right; the battle wasn't easy at all. We finally got custody of Cindy after a lot of time and money. Her mom was sure we had "stolen" her away. Barb couldn't understand that it had been Cindy's decision.

Having a brand new baby and a new teenager was not at all easy. I definitely had a few struggles with anxiety around this time. I remember turning to God and praying a lot. I loved Cindy and had always felt that Dale had received the bum end of the deal in that portion of his life. He had always called, cared for, and deeply loved Cindy. He had never missed a child support payment. However, Barb would often deny visits and phone calls when it suited her and blame Dale when Cindy would ask about it. When his ex-wife had asked if she could take Cindy to Texas when she was eight, he allowed it without making a big fuss, knowing how much he would miss his little girl. Dale had always done the right thing with regard to his daughter, and I was proud of him for this and loved him for it too. Years later, if God was wanting us to take care of this beautiful child, who was I to refuse?

We started attending the United Church in our community around the same time. I had long since opened my heart back up to God, but my life was becoming complicated, and I needed God more regularly in my life, along with the guidance of somebody (a minister) much more educated about his word than I. Our minister became an important part of our lives and our spiritual direction.

Cindy became a nice addition to our family. Some of the "teenage" issues were a bit hard for us to deal with so suddenly, but we tried our best. Jamilyn was in heaven, having shared her room with Cindy at the time. Cindy made new friends, adjusted well to a new school, and seemed happy. Her phone calls with her mother left Cindy feeling guilty and emotionally distraught. I had greatly wished I could have taken away some of Cindy's pain. We would have long talks about the situation.

Barb persevered and finally talked Cindy into coming home for a visit some ten months later. Cindy was very hesitant about the trip. We made sure we had all of the legal documents signed so her mom wouldn't try to keep her in Texas. However, all the documents in the world cannot change the direction God has on people's lives. Cindy never did return to live with us in Lac La Biche. Her mom had spoiled her rotten upon her return. She had redone her room and had manipulated her in many ways. She had stopped drinking, and that was good! However, Cindy was not returning to us, and we were heartbroken. Jamilyn's little heart just couldn't understand it, and neither could mine.

To compound the sadness we were feeling, Dale's mom had just passed away a few weeks earlier. It was such a shock as she had been in very good shape, physically. However, emotionally, she had been drained years before by a husband whose lifestyle indicated that alcohol was much more important than she was. We still miss Therese Marie Thody a great deal. What a lovely, giving, selfless woman. Poor Jamilyn had lost two very important people in her life within one month. My heart reached out to her.

We were suffering but still surviving. Our beautiful little baby girl, Kristy, innocently and wonderfully helped ease some of our pain. God had a different plan for our family than we realized.

Two months after Cindy went back to Texas, I discovered I was pregnant. After *almost* two vasectomies, God wanted this little one in our world. The gifts God gives are incredible. We just need to stop, look, and listen. He already knows our heart; we merely need to allow him in. With my third pregnancy, I became a bit scared. How could I cope with three children? How could we do this financially? There was a lot of worry, but I should have known better. God has helped us through it all. I put my faith in him.

Right around this time, we started attending a new church in town called the Evangelical Free Church. There have been two pastors working there since we started attending. They have both helped me and my family immensely through the last seven years. I am so blessed to be part of such a wonderful church! A month before our third child was born, my grandpa Rhyason died at the age of ninety-one, on March 19, the last day of *winter*. He had lived a long, healthy, and full life. He had been a farmer. We were very close, and I loved him so very much. I miss his big strong hands and awesome sense of humor! Not even a month later, my auntie Doris passed away after suffering from a long battle with a lung disease. This was the aunt I had lived with while going to college. What a wonderful, spiritual, giving lady. It was a very sad time, experiencing two great losses within a month!

Only nine days after my auntie passed away, on April 24, 2003, Jesse was born in Lac La Biche, Alberta. It was a time of renewal in our family after a lot of sadness. Jesse was a gift to us all, but I believe mostly to Dale, who had lost his daughter, again, only months before. He is our little miracle baby who was most definitely "meant to be"! I certainly cannot imagine my life without this beautiful, intelligent, loving child. God works in mysterious ways. He gives and takes away. Often even in our extreme pain, we are moving toward something good.

Now, in our lives today, we not only have two beautiful daughters, a handsome son, but an older daughter, Cindy, who loves us, wants us in her life, and keeps in close contact, though living in Texas. Cindy just had a brand new baby girl named Bailey Paige. She is engaged to be married next summer, on August 13, our anniversary! We are so happy for her. Her fiancée seems like a wonderful man.

Our lives have again become more colorful, as about one year ago, my nephew (Roni's son) Trevor came to live with us. He had been in a horrible car accident years before. Trevor was the driver, and one of his best friends was killed. Trevor had suffered a *great* deal psychologically. He was unable to cope with the enveloping negative emotions that surrounded the accident. Attempting to escape these feelings, he ended up coping in a negative fashion and got involved with a lot of drugs and alcohol. He was not doing well at all and had been unable to leave Calgary due to house arrest. Trevor sank deeper and deeper.

Finally it was time for a small family reunion up north at a campground near my house. We were celebrating my mom and auntie's birthdays. Trevor was finally allowed to leave the city with his parents after five years. Once he got away, and closer to the area where his friend (Boyle) had lived, he knew he didn't want to go back to the city and all its temptations. He said as much to his mom, and then she approached us. Dale and I were a bit hesitant at first, knowing the type of lifestyle Trevor had been leading. I mean, we had three children to consider. We talked, and we decided to allow Trevor to live with us under our conditions.

Trevor agreed and has been doing excellently! I am so very proud of the choices he's made and how far he has come in one year. He is working and making a good living. He is paying us rent and helping around the house. In May, he completed his first year of college to become an electrician, and he did marvelously! Trevor is so much fun to have around. He loves the kids and they love him back so much. Trevor loves to cook and he is very good, so I'm enjoying the breaks I get in the kitchen. All is well with our *new* blended family. We are blessed and thankful to have Trevor in our lives and to see how God's grace has worked in his life.

My older sister Roni has quit drinking for more than a year. She has lost about seventy pounds and is full of light and life. I am so thankful and proud of her too. My prayers since childhood have finally been answered! Roni is finally loving and taking care of herself. God has *his* own timing. Trevor and Roni have a wonderful relationship. It is the best relationship they have ever had, though it is long distance! God is good! My wonderful nephew Bryan, Trevor's younger brother, is living back at home with Roni and her husband, Ken, and he is finding his way.

An accident such as the one Trevor experienced does not merely affect the driver and those in the car at the time. Much more realistically, this tragedy was more like a rock thrown into a calm pond. The ripple effect caused many, many people to be hurt. Bryan was affected very directly by this accident. It was his older brother who was driving! Many of his friends were in the car that night too. Bryan is mourning a great deal of loss and change in his young life. When the accident happened, he was only seventeen. Obviously, Bryan didn't come out of this extremely difficult time unscathed. He quit school. He partied lots. He made some poor choices and he has suffered too. Bryan has so much potential to accomplish anything God may have in store for him. I believe in him and feel he is beginning to heal too.

My younger sister Tracey has recently gone through a divorce and is trying to cope with a very busy working life and taking care of two boys, one of whom is a teenager with ADHD. She has had a very difficult time lately, but I pray daily for her family and know there is hope for them too. My sweet nephew Kevin (age six) provides extra light for Tracey on her hardest days. Brayden, her oldest, just attended a camp for ADHD in Colorado and really learned a lot there too. Although Brayden has some challenges, as we all do, he has also been given many gifts, and I hope that through God's direction, he will come to realize and act on these gifts too.

My sisters have been an integral part of my life, and I love and appreciate them so very much. Our friendship is one of unconditional love and this is also how I feel about their families.

My mom and dad are thankfully very healthy and full of life. They travel, visit, babysit, golf, and camp. They spend six months in Arizona in the same trailer park my grandparents lived in years ago. Right now they are probably ready to see me as they have been watching our children while we are on holidays. We are so blessed to have them in our lives. They have continued to provide a foundation of support in my life, a foundation that can only have been built by God. I love them so much! My children will have grown much closer to my parents over the last two weeks. I can't wait to see everyone!

My life really has become quite colorful over the last few years, and I am thankful to God that he has given me an open mind. One cannot see color without light. My light is in Jesus, and through his guidance I have seen some miraculous things happen! There is a story in Genesis 37–47 about Joseph, who basically lived a life that took him from prison to palace. It is a very good story that I recommend you read. We focused on this story during our church's VBS (Vacation Bible School) week this summer. Because I was a family leader, I came to know the story quite well. I have been "imprisoned" many times and by many things in my life. Looking back, I was imprisoned by weight, acne, lust, alcohol, smoking, and most significantly, bipolar disorder. And yet today, I live in a palace! It may not be the same type of palace Joseph lived in, but I am truly blessed to live where I do in a beautiful home. I have an amazing family, immediate and extended. Wonderful friends also bless my palace. God has forgiven me. God's grace is amazing!

With regard to my bipolar, I am not cured but I have found

tools to help me live in freedom, most often. When I was diagnosed, no other family member had ever been diagnosed with bipolar. It is hereditary. It is a chemical imbalance of the brain. Symptoms often occur in later teens or early twenties. It can, however occur in childhood and is called early onset bipolar. It is a difficult disorder to diagnose. It can be masked as depression, ADHD, or schizophrenia. Through the years, I have managed to learn how to lead a good life. My recipe?

God (love) +Lithium + Balanced Lifestyle.

God has played such an amazing, encompassing role in my life as you have now read. Without his direction, grace, and love, I would not be here sharing my story. My relationship with God is extremely important and constant. Praying has become second nature to me, and I pray often throughout the day, often silently. I cannot fall asleep without praying about other people, counting my blessings, or asking for wisdom. Many nights I fall asleep during prayer. The power of prayer in my life, as with anyone who truly believes, is absolutely incredible.

Lithium has been a topic repeated numerous times in my story. It has been a gift from God to me. Without this medication, there is no way I would be functioning the way I am—believe me, I've tried! I am so thankful for the help that this little capsule gives me and my family.

For me, a balanced lifestyle includes healthy eating, enough sleep, working, playing, the occasional glass of wine, and exercise. Living up north, I also add vitamin D in the winter to help with the lack of sunshine being absorbed. Vitamin D can also be a factor in depression for many people, especially in the winter. Occasionally (once or twice monthly at the most), I feel my motor really running, and I feel anxious and irritable. I have found that clonazepam works amazingly to quickly calm my nerves and let me breathe deeply again. I take only half a tablet (.25mg) and soon feel capable of handling my day; it is helpful to me on my roughest days. It causes no drowsiness or any bad side effects. Usually the hardest days occur just before or the day of my period. I am extremely grateful to have all these things available to me to help me function better. I am long past worrying that maybe I shouldn't take anything for anxiety. If there is help, take it! Why put myself, the ones I love, and people around me through my extreme crankiness when there is something to help? That being said, there are some medications that can cause addiction for some people, so a person must be careful. This has never been an issue for me, and I can go two or three months without even requiring one tablet!

Balance and lifestyle are also about relationships. Looking back at my track record with men, this may be hard to believe, but I have been completely faithful to my husband for eighteen years, which, of course, is a portion of my balanced lifestyle, and I am thankful for God helping me overcome this particular "addiction." Relationships with friends, coworkers, and family are also important to me. Being able to talk, share, laugh, poke fun at yourself, and not be judged is very therapeutic, and I am blessed to have some amazing people in my life.

If you are struggling with this disorder, or someone close to you has shown signs of having this disorder, I pray for you all. I pray that you may use this recipe in your own life to help you cope and learn to love yourself and to love living again. As with any recipe, you may need to adjust the ingredients somewhat to suit your specific condition. I can only hope these words have somehow given *you* a ray of light … a flicker of hope!

I, the Lord, have called you and given you power …
you will open the eyes of the blind and set free those
who sit in dark prisons. —Isaiah 42:6–7 (CEV)

Acknowledgments

I am so very thankful to all of the doctors, nurses, and professional staff who helped me reclaim myself physically and mentally.

I am extremely grateful for my close friends who believe in me and love me as a *person*, not a disorder. More specifically, I want to thank Lisa Funk who many years ago learned about my condition, loved me anyway, and inspired me to one day write about it. Thank you to Crystal Cardinal, who is a very close friend, who listened to me, encouraged me, and was the first to preview my book. I am very thankful to my friend Shelley Erick who always listens without judgment and with an incredibly caring heart. Thank you to my musical friend who always makes me laugh and has encouraged me to think and live outside the box.

I am so very grateful for a young lady who came into my life and helped me so selflessly with my book. Thank you, Jenna Parsons, for all of your time, suggestions, and care in editing my book. You were amazing!

I am also thankful to the open-minded parents of my students who, having known about my condition, allowed me to teach their children anyway.

Thank you to my mom, dad and sisters who somehow loved me when I wasn't loveable at all; who helped me dearly in my darkest times; who helped me see the light! I love you all so much!

I am truly grateful for my immediate family: Dale, Jamilyn, Kristy, and Jesse. You are all a true blessing to me. You all give me a true purpose, and I love you all so dearly. My family reinforces my daily decision to continue taking my lovely orange and white capsules of sanity and to try my hardest to live a Christian life. I need to stay healthy for me and for all of you!

My greatest thanks go out to God because without his direction, unconditional love, grace, and guidance I wouldn't be here today, and I certainly wouldn't have been brave enough to write this message. God is great!

About the Author

Shelley Thody is happily married with three amazing children, ages fifteen, eleven, and nine. Her beautiful grandchildren, ages four and two, live in Texas with their parents.

When considering the mental health journey she's been on, it truly amazes her how God's love has forgiven her and blessed her with such an abundance of riches. Being a teacher and a Christian, she felt compelled to share her story—to shed light on those suffering. Shelley currently lives in Alberta, Canada.

CPSIA information can be obtained at www.ICGtesting.com
Printed in the USA
LVOW041953030113

314265LV00001B/2/P